SELLING ENERGY

INSPIRING IDEAS THAT GET MORE PROJECTS APPROVED!

VOLUME 1

Enjoy + Prosper!

MARK **JEWELL**

WITH RACHEL **CHRISTENSON**

SELLING ENERGY:
Inspiring Ideas That Get More Projects Approved!

www.SellingEnergy.com

Interior design: Adina Cucicov at Flamingo Designs

ISBN: 978-1-941991-00-8

DEDICATION

This book would not have been conceived, much less written, had it not been for my family. My father gave me the drive to succeed… my late mother, the sense of humor to prevail. My wife continues to create new avenues for delivering our message. Our children, Jane Lumen and Jack Mason, keep us laughing and give us a powerful reason to focus on making the world a better place.

I would also like to thank Michael Bannett for helping us produce the Jewell Insights™ daily blog and ESP Ninja™ smartphone app that provide thousands of professionals with a dose of energy-focused inspiration on a daily basis.

Finally, I'd like to thank our many followers who pause long enough to keep us posted on how they are applying our ideas to advance their personal and professional success.

TABLE OF CONTENTS

SELLING ENERGY

INSPIRING IDEAS THAT **GET MORE PROJECTS APPROVED!**

VOLUME 1

MARK **JEWELL**

WITH RACHEL **CHRISTENSON**

PREFACE

"The best way to prosper yourself is to prosper others."
WALTER JEWELL

The first time I heard that advice, I was a very young man sitting at the dinner table with my family. The topic that particular night was some variation of "What would you like to be when you grow up?" After hearing my first few ideas, my father shared his simple ten-word suggestion for how to enjoy not only a successful career, but also personal fulfillment.

Today, the lobby of our San Francisco headquarters features an Inspiration Wall that prominently displays my father's wise words and many others like them. That wall is the touchstone of what my team and I do every day. We teach fellow professionals how to enjoy greater success in their worlds by making others more successful.

"Learning to sell efficiency effectively" is a phrase we use quite often in our work. Having witnessed efficiency decision-making in more than three billion square feet of real estate over the last twenty years, we've found that very few people actually know how to *sell* efficiency. Most people simply *promote* it, as if it were a greater good like finding a cure for cancer or housing the homeless. In some circles, the concept of "promoting" efficiency is so pervasive, you'd think "sell" was a four-letter word!

Many people are not very comfortable "selling," even in settings where the notion of selling is not taboo. Why? For one, the average salesperson receives less than three days of sales training in his or her entire career. Moreover, most of that is really *product knowledge training* rather than teaching someone *how to sell.*

Second, many sales training programs feature techniques that are no longer effective given the increased sophistication and access to information that today's buyers bring to the table.

Finally, most sales training programs are one-size-fits-all, as if one could sell efficiency the same way one might sell real estate, insurance, or photocopiers. Without a doubt, the efficiency industry needs to stop promoting its wares and start selling them. In order for that to happen, many market actors will need training on *how to sell efficiency effectively.*

The Efficiency Sales Professional Institute is not about "drop and run" training where folks attend a fast-paced seminar to get motivated and educated, only to revert to their old attitudes and habits shortly thereafter. All of our offerings are designed with an eye toward "drip-irrigation" content reinforcement to ensure that lessons learned are consistently applied to drive more sales and move efficiency forward.

Jewell Insights™ is a perfect example of this philosophy. Every day of the year, we publish a short essay via our free ESP Ninja™ App and email blog. Each essay either introduces or expands on a topic covered in our in-person and online offerings. Our workshops offer a wide range of innovative mindsets, strategies, and tactics for selling efficiency effectively. Jewell Insights provides daily reinforcement that helps those innovations "stick."

In the words of Mike Rowe (of *Dirty Jobs* fame), "Innovation without imitation is a total waste of time." Our combination of *revelation* and *repetition* transforms ordinary salespeople into lifelong efficiency sales professionals. On a related note, one of my favorite quotes is, "Successful people do what unsuccessful people are unwilling to do." To be successful, you need more than a good idea. Turning a vision into a reality requires real work.

Many of our subscribers have already shared how applying something they read in Jewell Insights allowed them to triumph in a sales situation, so it was an easy decision to compile some of our favorite essays into a book that would benefit an even larger audience.

You may elect to read this book from start to finish. Or you might turn to an essay at random when you need a dose of inspiration. Either way, we're confident you'll find plenty of insights that will help you prosper yourself by prospering others.

YOU MUST BE A SALES PROFESSIONAL

Most organizations seeking to advance the sale of efficiency projects have widely varying staff roles supporting their mission. Utilities have account execs, program designers, program managers, third-party program management contractors, trade allies, program evaluators, and so on. Mechanical service contractors have business development staff, inside sales staff, dispatchers, and field techs.

So how many roles in these and similar organizations really need to understand how to sell efficiency effectively? *More than you might think.*

I like to start any discussion of selling efficiency more effectively with the following three guiding principles:

- Energy efficiency products, services, and programs all require effective selling.
- Professional sales skills will help you advance efficiency, regardless of your role in the process.
- You can be a sales professional even if your job title does not include the word "sales."

Frankly, anyone in your organization who works with customers needs to understand efficiency-focused professional selling. They will uncover plenty of needs if they know what to look for, what questions to ask, how to field the customer's questions, and how to migrate a conversation from a service call to an exploration of how enhanced efficiency could make the customer's operation more competitive, profitable, and valuable. Moreover, their input will help you triangulate the organization's requirements so that you'll be more knowledgeable when your actual business development person ultimately connects with whatever person on your customer's staff has the final say on which products and services they will buy from you.

On a related note, one of the hallmarks of sales professionalism is the ability to move from "reactive" to "proactive" sales. Can you really grow your business by simply fielding calls and producing estimates upon request? By the time you hear about a project using this approach, you are often too late. There are several dimensions of being proactive:

- Coaching others in the decision chain to drive requests for premium approaches.
- Communicating compelling value propositions that preempt value engineering.
- Selling directly to the owner.

If you are proactive in developing *interest in* and *demand for* higher-efficiency approaches, you will be paving the way toward increased sales. Getting to the owner and communicating how your solution makes his or her life easier or more profitable sets the stage for more effective selling later on.

By the way, having utility account reps, field service techs, and other non-traditional selling roles trained in efficiency-focused professional selling yields another vital advantage. It gives you the insight you need to take threads of information returned to you from your "field operatives" and craft them into proactive and compelling messages that will create demand for your offerings from the top of your prospect's organization. That "intel from the field" will also help you identify all of the players whose endorsement you will need to "soft-circle" prior to going to top management with a plan you feel confident will win organization-wide approval.

"All successful people are big dreamers.
They imagine what their future could be, ideal in every
respect, and then they work every day toward their distant
vision, that goal or purpose."
BRIAN TRACY

DO YOUR BROCHURES DRIVE PROSPECTS TO EMBRACE EFFICIENCY?

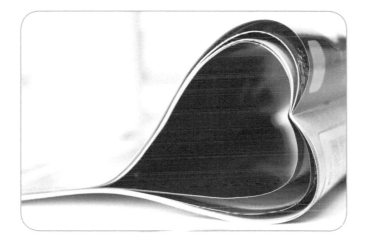

How often do brochures make prospects fall in love with efficiency? What would you say if I told you that, more often than not, brochures get in the way of an effective conversation with your prospect? Why? Because in most cases, the marketing department is totally out of sync with the sales department in terms of what should be included in those brochures in the first place.

Ask yourself: Are your marketing and sales departments—in fact, is your entire organization—capable of resonating at the frequency of your prospect? Has anyone in your organization taken the time to develop

a genuinely nuanced understanding of how efficiency resonates with that prospect's reality at the four distinct levels that matter: the segment, the industry, the organization, and the prospect's own role within that organization?

Do your brochures contain any mention of how efficiency is going to produce benefits that are meaningful at each of these four levels? If not, I would respectfully suggest that your brochures are not worth printing, much less introducing into a conversation with your prospect.

"For every sale you miss because you're too enthusiastic, you will miss a hundred because you're not enthusiastic enough."

ZIG ZIGLAR

DO THICK PROPOSALS DRIVE PROSPECTS TO EMBRACE EFFICIENCY?

How often do weighty "free audits," detailed technical studies, or long-winded proposals drive customers to embrace efficiency? How many times in your career have you either offered one of these things to a prospect or received one yourself with horror, realizing that now you have to read the thing or at least pretend you did?

Tom Sant is a nationally respected consultant and author who spends his life coaching people on how to make more effective proposals. I was presenting at a national conference where he was also speaking and overheard him telling his audience, "You could probably put the words

'Up yours!' anywhere in a thick proposal like this and never be called out because people simply don't read them!"

I have to agree with him, particularly in situations where you and several other bidders are responding to a Request for Proposal. The committee (or, worse yet, individual) responsible for reviewing submittals might have twenty or more of these boat anchors arriving in the mail. With only a week or two to review and comment on each and every one of them, do you think those proposals ever get read? Skimmed, perhaps. Read from cover to cover? Not on your life.

Let's say one respondent took a different tack, submitting a one-page proposal (in keeping with the techniques taught in the Efficiency Sales Professional™ and Learning to S.E.E.: Sell Efficiency Effectively™ courses) that explained his or her approach to the project, along with a separate technical appendix containing the necessary details. Whose bid response would be reviewed first? Whose bid response would be the most memorable? Whose bid would be the first to be discussed when the committee met to compare notes on all submittals?

"Don't judge each day by the harvest you reap but by the seeds that you plant."
ROBERT LOUIS STEVENSON

DO ENVIRONMENTAL CONCERNS DRIVE PROSPECTS TO EMBRACE EFFICIENCY?

If you got into this business because you wanted to save the environment, you might want to keep your agenda to yourself in certain settings. I remember reading a study published by the National Academy of Sciences in 2013. The experiment compared the reactions of various ideology buyers who were each given the opportunity to purchase a conventional lamp or a higher first-cost, premium-efficiency one. When faced with those two alternatives, one of which was three times more expensive, an equal number of moderates and conservatives purchased the higher-efficiency lamp, using its savings over time to justify the additional cost. However, when the researchers repeated the test and

placed a pro-environment sticker on the same higher-first-cost lamp, sales among conservatives plummeted.

The researchers concluded that connecting energy-efficient products to environmental concerns can negatively affect the demand for these products, especially among persons in the United States who are more politically conservative. They added, "Although the majority of participants, regardless of ideology, selected the more expensive energy-efficient light bulb when it was unlabeled, the more moderate and conservative participants were less likely to purchase this option when an environmental label was attached to it."

On a related note, I remember hearing a particularly skeptical prospect declare that as soon as he heard environmentalists telling stories of "polar bears drowning because of shrinking ice caps," he refused to believe anything else they had said. He continued by explaining that he had just returned from Sea World where he saw polar bears swimming with beach balls on their noses. "Polar bears can swim, for goodness sake, and if they're lying about the polar bears drowning in the Artic, they must be lying about a lot of other things!"

"Act as if what you do makes a difference. It does."
WILLIAM JAMES

HOW OFTEN DOES "SAVING MONEY" DRIVE THE DECISION?

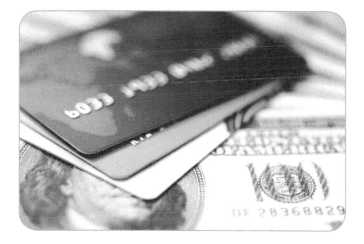

How often does the promise of saving money drive decisions? Well, let me rephrase that. Here in America, are we known as being a nation of savers? I don't think so. If we were, our cumulative credit card debt wouldn't have tripled since 1994.

So what makes you think that when your prospects go to their offices, all of a sudden they become very careful with their money—or with their boss' money? In fact, it's even worse because at the office they're spending someone else's money. Just be careful about assuming that, "Oh, but look

at all the money we're going to save you in lower utility bills!" is going to be the close that's going to get the deal done.

On a related note, there is a considerable amount of research out there suggesting that folks value avoidance of loss more heavily than the promise of gain. If avoided utility expense is the crux of your benefits list, you might consider rephrasing this to communicate avoiding a serious loss rather than capturing a windfall.

"A successful business creates a network that is an inch wide and a mile deep, not a mile wide and an inch deep."
DAVID ALEXANDER

ARE YOU EVEN FOCUSING ON THE RIGHT SAVINGS?

If you want to capture the attention of a busy executive with the prospect of improving his building's energy-related systems, should you focus your "elevator pitch" and "one-page proposal" on projected savings in kilowatt-hours, therms, or utility expenses? Or should you focus on something else that's nearer and dearer to your executive's heart and probably likely to "move the needle" in a more significant way? Consider the following assumptions in the context of a typical open-office workspace:

- $40,000 average salary and benefits per person.
- 200 square feet per person.
- $200 per square foot in payroll vs. $2 per square foot in utilities.

What if your efficiency campaign boosted productivity by just 1 percent?

Assume that your average office employee makes $40,000 per year and sits on a floor that's been designed to accommodate five people per thousand square feet. That's $40,000 divided by 200 square feet, or $200 per square foot in payroll. What's your utility bill? If yours is an average office building in the continental United States, it's probably around $2 per square foot. That means that your payroll is *one hundred times as large as your utility bill* on a per-square-foot basis. If you're a manager, what should *you* be focusing on: your utility bill or your payroll expense?

Let's say you're selling an energy-efficiency upgrade that is expected to have a positive impact on occupant comfort or convenience. Think about it—on most tenant satisfaction surveys, "too hot/too cold" appears at or near the top of the list of tenant concerns. Could a new direct digital control system make people more thermally comfortable?

What about lighting quality? Would your energy-efficient lighting system reduce glare? Or improve the quality of lighting so that the occupants working under it are better able to do their jobs? Perhaps less eye strain? Fewer headaches? Fewer mistakes?

What if you sell window films that reduce the heat and glare of the afternoon sun on the south and west-facing sides of a commercial office building? Might the workers in perimeter offices be at least one percent more effective if they didn't need to squint with the sun in their eyes for an hour or more in the afternoon?

Do any of these upgrades have the potential to improve the productivity of building occupants by at least 1 percent? Before you answer that question, let's think about what a *1 percent* improvement would entail. If you do the math, you'll realize that if an office worker present for ten hours a day is able to work an additional *six minutes a day* as a result of an improvement you make to his/her workspace, you will have accomplished a 1 percent productivity uptick.

Six minutes a day. The last time I looked, six minutes was equivalent to two turns of one of those Williams-Sonoma sand-filled hourglass timers that signal a perfectly cooked soft-boiled egg! Two turns of a tiny hourglass egg timer. That's all it takes.

Do you think a person that has to leave his or her desk and go to the break room to get a cup of tea or coffee to warm up because the workplace is overly air-conditioned wastes more or less than six minutes a day doing so?

And what if they stop by someone else's desk to kvetch about the temperature? Maybe their colleague joins them for the coffee break. Maybe the coffee is so lousy, they leave the building together and go to Starbucks to warm up. How many minutes of productivity would *that* waste?

By the way, in case you think this is too fanciful a value proposition to sway a jaded executive's decision-making process, you'll be interested to hear a story that one of our ninjas recently shared with me. He was interested in selling an HVAC replacement project valued at $1.6 million to a highly occupied building that was having both maintenance and comfort problems. His prospect preferred a quick fix that would only solve the most critical comfort problems and cost almost a million dollars less.

When our well-trained sales professional was invited by senior management to present the alternatives so that they could determine which of these two paths the company would be approving, he came prepared with some very interesting non-utility-cost financial savings data in his back pocket. He first described to senior management the costs and implications of each of the two solutions. He paused, and then casually added that if the more expensive system produced as little as *1.2 minutes of additional productivity per day* for each of the workers occupying that facility, the value of the productivity savings would equal the value of the $1.6 million project's annual energy savings!

After a half-minute or so of silence, the most senior executive in the room said, "That can't be right." Rather than protesting, the sales professional simply replied, "How do you mean?" The executive continued, "It has to be at least a five-minute daily comfort advantage." After a few more minutes of discussion, the exec directed his staff to prepare the paperwork needed for him to approve the larger project.

The moral of the story? There are three categories of benefits: utility-cost financial, non-utility-cost financial, and non-financial. An efficiency sales professional carefully considers each and every one of these benefit categories in order to present a proposed project in its most favorable light.

"Character consists of what you do on the third and fourth tries."

JAMES MICHENER

DO PEOPLE REALLY DECIDE OR SIMPLY COMPARE?

Attend our efficiency-focused professional sales training and you'll hear me say over and over, "Most people don't make decisions. They make comparisons. And it's up to you to frame the comparison properly."

Dan Ariely, an internationally renowned behavioral economist and author of two New York Times bestselling books, *Predictably Irrational* and *The Upside of Irrationality*, has done extensive research on how people make decisions. In his TED Talk called, "Are we in control of our own decisions?" he presents several examples of decision-making scenarios that clearly demonstrate how significantly a selection can be swayed by

the context and arrangement of possible choices. This eye-opener is one of several featured videos in our Efficiency Sales Professional™ Certificate Boot Camp, and if you haven't viewed it already, I recommend you do so.

There are countless examples of how this concept of "decision vs. comparison" plays out in the context of getting efficiency projects approved.

Let's start with the simplest case. Assume your prospect asks, "What's the payback period?" and you respond, "Three years." What comparison is that prospect making in his mind? "Well, I have my money in my pocket now, and it feels comforting having access to that capital. If I do the investment you're proposing, I'll have to wait three years to get my money back. Uh, no thanks."

But what if the prospect had asked, "What's the Return on Investment (ROI)?" You respond, "33 percent." Now what comparison is the prospect making in his head? "Wow, I just returned from my bank and noticed that they were paying 3 percent on a 36-month CD. This investment is eleven times that." Now, there is an inherent fallacy in comparing the ROI of an expense-reducing capital project with the rate of return on a federally insured CD; however, plenty of decision-makers feel totally comfortable using such "apples and kiwi" comparisons when making decisions.

I'll give you an even crazier example. Years ago, I was presenting a project to a prospect. He asked me, somewhat accusingly, "What's the payback?" As soon as I responded, "3.2 years," he started shaking his head wildly as if he were being attacked by a swarm of angry bees! "No way. We don't do any projects around here with paybacks over three years. I'm sorry. We just don't do it." At that point, I responded with a softening statement, the conjunction "and" (not "but"), and what I call a "pattern interrupt."

I said, "John, I understand. And, I think what you'll find more interesting is that this investment sports a Return on Investment of more than 30 percent per year." As soon as he heard "30 percent" his eyes widened. He leaned forward and said, "Now *that's* a figure that would make my capital budgeting folks warm and cozy. Tell me more."

Yes, that really happened. All the more proof that people don't make decisions. They make comparisons. And efficiency sales professionals know that it is their responsibility to frame the comparison to make it obvious that saying "yes" to your project is the most rational (or predictably irrational) thing that your prospect can do.

"High achievers spot rich opportunities swiftly,
make big decisions quickly and move into action immediately.
Follow these principles and you can make
your dreams come true."
ROBERT SCHULLER

THE TROUBLE WITH TALKING TECH

KILOWATTHOURS

When I was a very young man selling efficiency solutions for the first time, I got lucky and managed to land an appointment with the CFO of a Fortune 500 company. I knew that if I convinced this CFO to let us do lighting retrofits for his national portfolio of properties, it would be a game changer for my company.

So I get an appointment with this chap. His assistant asks me to "make myself comfortable" in the biggest boardroom I had ever seen—complete with a fifty-foot-long endangered tropical hardwood table and three dozen overstuffed leather swivel chairs to boot, each with a leather blotter and crystal water goblet placed neatly in front of it. Oh, and plenty of oil portraits of presumably deceased corporate founders covering the walls.

The CFO finally arrives, about thirty minutes late for our meeting. He is a caricature of a Fortune 500 accounting head: razor-cut hair… a heavily starched, white button-down Oxford shirt and Ivy League rep tie; wing tips so highly polished that they could be used as mirrors to signal passing planes; yellow legal pad, HP12C calculator, and 0.5mm mechanical pencil clenched firmly in hand. He strides confidently into the room and, in true New York City rapport-building fashion, slaps his legal pad on the table, tosses his calculator and mechanical pencil down onto it, and simply says, "Hit me."

Realizing that this chap is a no-nonsense guy, I launch right into it—all the technical specifications of lighting increases I could imagine giving his buildings, the improved color rendering index and chromaticity of my proposed retrofits, the whole nine yards. About ten minutes into the pitch, he stops me. He picks up his mechanical pencil for the first time, puts its point to paper, and says, "What was that last term you just used?"

I say, "Chromaticity?" He says, "Yeah, that's it. How do you spell it?" So I spell it, and he writes it down. "Now what exactly does it mean?" I recite the textbook definition of "chromaticity," practically verbatim out of the Illuminating Engineering Society of North America's Lighting Handbook. He studiously copies my description word for word, then sets his pencil back down on his legal pad and says, "Thank you. Go on."

I say, "Excuse me, but of everything I've told you so far today, 'chromaticity' seems to be the only term that caught your fascination. Why is that?" He looks down, seemingly a little bit embarrassed, and then confesses, "My eleven-year-old daughter and I have a little word game we play at dinner every night, and I'm fairly confident I'm going to get her with 'chromaticity' tonight, so for that I thank you. Now go on."

That's about as much as any non-lighting-industry CFO cares about chromaticity. Would "chromaticity" ultimately convince this particular

CFO to invest in a portfolio-wide lighting retrofit? Absolutely not. After that meeting I was so miffed, I wanted to look up his home telephone number, call his daughter after I figured she'd be home from school, and say something like, "Listen smarty pants, you don't know me, and don't ask me how I know this, but your father is going to hit you with 'chromaticity' tonight at dinner. This is *exactly* how you spell it, and this is *exactly* what it means, and *don't* tell him that anyone called!" But alas, I didn't do it. I had learned my lesson, and that was sufficiently satisfying.

Why am I sharing this story? Because far too many people who actually land the coveted C-level meeting wind up squandering it by focusing on the technical aspects of what they sell. Why do they take this approach? Because most people in sales receive less than three days of professional sales training in their entire career and most of that is *product knowledge* training. They actually think that the way to sell stuff is to tell people everything they know about their products and that doing so will make it obvious to their prospects that they should buy. Guess what? *That approach accomplishes exactly the opposite result.*

The more information you shower on a prospect, the *worse* your chances are of closing a sale. As you blather on about all of the technical details, the prospect gets into deeper and deeper and deeper water. At some point, they realize they can no longer touch the bottom of the pool. Their inner voice starts saying, "I'm in way over my head. This is turning out to be a much more complicated conversation than I thought we would be having. I'd better call in some technical experts who can tell me whether or not this salesperson really knows what he's talking about."

The moral of the story? Unless you're interested in giving your prospects some fodder for dinnertime word games with their children, forget the technical jargon and focus on your prospect's story, not yours.

"REAL TALK" TRUMPS "SMALL TALK"

L et's assume you're meeting a new prospect for your efficiency offerings. What steps should you take to ensure that you're as prepared as possible for a meaningful discussion that produces an actionable outcome?

For most "salespeople," the answer is some variant of the following four steps:

1. Show up for the meeting.
2. Ask predictable opening questions to assess the prospect's needs and/or interest in your offering.

3. Modify your "pitch" based on the answers you hear in Step 2.
4. Hope for the best.

If I had to describe the above-referenced approach in two words, it would be "winging it."

Unfortunately, "winging it" most often produces suboptimal results. It squanders valuable meeting time on questions that could have (and should have) been answered with a little pre-meeting research. Moreover, it gives the salesperson very little time to customize his or her approach to capitalize on the prospect's answers.

Sales professionals approach this challenge differently. They take the time to research their prospect before the meeting. Where does the organization stand on the topic of improving its energy efficiency? Which players' cooperation will you need? Construction? Design? Finance? Maintenance? Sustainability? What names are associated with each of those roles? How well do they work together? Do they have a reputation for collaborating professionally or hiding in their respective silos?

How do you acquire such insights? Talk to people in your network who may know them. Look them up on LinkedIn, Facebook, or Twitter. Google them thoroughly, looking for articles they have written or articles in which they've been quoted. Look for committees on which they serve, national associations to which they belong, things that have been said about them in the news. Simply put, look for any information that helps you understand their backgrounds, preferences, biases toward or against enhanced efficiency, etc.

Pay particular attention to anything that provides insight into the personalities involved. The information you assemble becomes the fuel for what I call "real talk" once you get face-to-face with the prospect.

Let me give you a real-life example. Last year, one of my larger utility clients asked me to reach out to a customer who controlled a large portfolio of high-energy-intensity buildings. The utility had noted that, although this portfolio had tremendous potential for upgrades, it had not participated in any of the utility's rebate or incentive programs. The utility thought that if I met with this company's CEO, I could help them understand why efficiency had not been a higher priority for this customer.

So what did I do? The night before my scheduled meeting with the CEO, I did some research. In under two hours, I discovered that he was a larger-than-life character with a somewhat checkered past. In fact, he had become involved in some real "urinary Olympics" with neighbors and code officials alike. A common theme emerged from all of the articles I had read: This CEO was an absolute megalomaniac. It's not uncommon for a real estate CEO to be a megalomaniac. It takes a lot of drive and ego to build the sort of specialty portfolio that this man now controlled.

The following day, I drove to the customer's headquarters to meet with the CEO. The traffic was terrible. It was raining so hard that had I been Noah, I would have started building my Ark! Oh, and just to make things more interesting, the headquarters was surrounded by multiple construction zones, which eliminated virtually all of the street parking.

Fortunately, I always try to arrive thirty minutes early, so even with the traffic, weather, and parking challenges, I still arrived on time. What happened next was a direct result of the research I had done the night before.

I walked into the boardroom where the CEO had just finished an earlier meeting. Did I complain about the weather? No. Did I whine about the lack of parking? No. Did I talk about anything other than him? No. The first thing I said was, "John (not his real name), I really like what you said last April about the resilience of your property type in today's real estate economy." He smiled broadly and asked, "What did I say?" I replied, "You said that regardless of the state of the economy, your particular property type would escape unscathed because there's consistent need for the kind of facilities you specialize in. And you know something? You're absolutely right. My partners and I had a two-million-square-foot portfolio in Southern California in the late Eighties, and because of how careful we were in selecting properties, we effectively insulated ourselves from the economic hardships that defined the early Nineties." He said (still beaming), "Where did I say that?" I said, "I believe it was the *Business Journal* last April." He said, "Oh yeah, I remember that interview. Come on in, sit down. What did you want to chat about today?"

So what happened in those first few seconds? My hunch is that he expected some energy-efficiency geek to arrive with an armful of utility brochures on rebates and incentives. Instead, he was pleasantly surprised to meet a peer, someone who really understood his industry—and, perhaps more importantly, someone who respected him as a sharp real estate investor.

He probably appreciated the fact that I had taken the time to research and remember what he had said in an interview.

Those first few minutes of "real talk" framed the conversation we were about to have on the important role that energy efficiency could play in making his portfolio even more valuable.

True sales professionals are astute enough to realize that traffic, weather, parking, or similar small talk wastes valuable "first impression" time. They realize how powerful "real talk" can be in setting the stage for a productive meeting. Moreover, they're willing to invest the time up front to ensure that the "real talk" is absolutely spot-on.

CONNECTING THE DOTS
DRIVES SALES

One of the most important attributes of a true sales professional is the ability to tell the prospect's story rather than his own. He then connects the dots in new and creative ways so the prospect realizes the link between what is being sold and what the prospect is seeking—to move beyond features, and even beyond benefits, into *values* that the prospect really cares about.

Think about it. Your prospects are consumed with *their* industries, not yours. They don't need to understand your technology or even your industry to buy from you. They need to feel comfortable that you understand *their* situation, what drives value in *their* world, and that your recommendations will get them closer to *where they already know they want to go.*

I often say that your sales success will be directly correlated with your ability to connect the dots between the benefits your offering can deliver and the *yardsticks your prospects are already using to measure their success.*

Your prospects are not waking up in the morning thinking, "Wow, I hope I can save some kilowatt-hours or therms today!" Or, "Boy, if I only had another couple hundred control points in my energy management system, my life would be complete!"

What *are* they thinking about when they get dressed for work in the morning?

- Keeping their staffs happy and productive.
- Keeping tenant hot/cold calls to a minimum.
- Coming up with an "edge" that will allow them to fill those last 50,000 square feet of vacancy.
- Finding a way to boost their retail sales per square foot to keep the Wall Street analysts happy.

You get the idea. They're probably *not* thinking about static pressure, delta T, chromaticity, color rendering index, or any of the other technical jargon that salespeople often lapse into.

And remember, you need to connect the dots at many levels:

- Segment-specific
- Organizational
- Professional
- Personal

MOTIVATION, NOT EDUCATION

Do you ever wonder why energy-efficiency reports are so long? Moreover, do you ever wonder if anyone actually reads them?

Tony Robbins is fond of saying that the quality of your life is directly related to the quality of the questions you ask. So here's a more useful question for you to consider:

Do you want your readers to learn something new and interesting, or do you want them to *be motivated to take action*?

It is my studied observation over the last two decades that most people who intend to write energy-efficiency proposals actually wind up writing reports instead. This causes them to adopt the persona of a "building scientist" or "educator"—as if their prospect actually had the time or even the interest to suffer through 100 or more pages and learn some new information. One need only witness the infinitesimally small percentage of these reports that make it to implementation to realize that this is a broken model.

This topic of focusing on motivation rather than education should inform all of our outbound communication. Whether it's a phone call, a voicemail, an email, a report, a proposal, or a presentation, first decide on the goal. What do you want your prospect to do in the end? If you identify your one primary intention, you're ahead of the game. And if you continue coming back to that theme—just as a piece of music always returns to its refrain—you will reinforce that primary intention and motivate your audience to take the action you desire.

"Only those who have learned the power of sincere and selfless contribution experience life's deepest joy: true fulfillment."
TONY ROBBINS

SALES PROFESSIONAL AS SYMPHONY CONDUCTOR

When planning your strategy for closing the complex sale, one of the first questions you need to ask is, "How many stakeholders will be involved in the buying process—either as an initiator, a gatekeeper, an influencer, a decision-maker, a procurement specialist, or an end user?" (Those six classifications are the subject of an insightful *Harvard Business Review* article called, "Major Sales: Who Really Does the Buying?")

The next question you need to answer is, "What does each of these stakeholders value?"

The third and final question to ponder is, "How can I reframe my proposal so that it resonates with those values?"

Pursuing these three steps in this order will equip you with the insights you need to soft-circle approval of all players before you seek to close the sale.

By the way, imagine what would happen if you *didn't* take the time to understand what each of these people thought about energy efficiency. What if you did what most salespeople do and tried to sell a single stakeholder on the energy efficiency improvement? Ask yourself a simple question: Do you really want the success of your sales process to hinge on that one person's ability to translate and communicate your value proposition to everybody else around that table? Realize that your internal champion cannot approve, fund, and implement the project alone. If you sidestep your responsibility to do all of the selling, your outcome will be largely dependent on the uncertain ability of someone else to sell your project for you. Are you willing to take that risk?

Let's assume you're trying to sell an energy upgrade to a multi-tenant commercial building, and your initial point of contact is the property manager. Few property managers can unilaterally decide to move forward with a major energy project. The manager has to convince the budgeting folks to authorize the capital. He or she has to convince the engineering staff that the project will not have any deleterious impacts on the building's mechanical systems. The manager also needs to convince the tenants that any temporary inconvenience caused by the installation is worth enduring. If capital cost recovery language will be used to recoup the landlord's investment in the upgrade by clawing back some or all of the utility savings, the tenants also need to be briefed on how that process will work. And they need to be assured that doing the project makes sense, even though they may not see any real savings for several years while the resulting utility bill reductions are being diverted to amortize the initial investment (plus interest in some cases).

Sales professionals are like symphony conductors. The quality of the music they produce is a direct consequence of the collaboration between their players. The more they understand who those players are, what each values, and what each is capable of contributing, the sweeter their music (i.e., their deal flow) will be.

> *"Sometimes one creates a dynamic impression by saying something, and sometimes one creates as significant an impression by remaining silent."*
> DALAI LAMA

NO PLAYER TOO SMALL

Salespeople often complain about not being able to connect with higher-level decision-makers at networking events and trade shows. Sales professionals know that it often doesn't matter. Here's why…

Assume an organization that you've been researching takes the time to participate in a networking event or trade show. However, since the C-level execs are often too busy to attend, they send their "delegates"— mid-level execs who can, among other things, represent the organization and report back on who else was there. In many cases, these delegates will be fairly low on the totem pole—perhaps even interns or brand-new hires. It's unlikely they'll have a full picture of the organization's needs, much less the ability to approve a proposal from you. However, they may have valuable insights into the company, including which players would likely be involved in evaluating your offerings. Bottom line: If approached with respect and decorum, these non-decision-makers may provide a fast track to the right people.

Here's how this phenomenon plays out in real life: Suppose you're at a conference or networking event. You scan the room for "decision-makers." What you see instead are small clusters of people standing in the corners like nervous adolescents at a high school dance. They are used to being ignored because they don't have a lot of clout within their own organizations. They may be there because their boss told them to attend.

A "salesperson" would ignore these folks as not having the power to effect change. A sales professional knows otherwise. He approaches as many of these delegates as possible. He asks them how long they've been with their respective companies, how they're enjoying the experience thus far, and what they actually do day to day. Note the order and tone of the questions: Each interaction is a human conversation, not some cold-call qualification script being acted out in person.

If you take this approach, each of your conversation partners will eventually ask, "So what do you do?" At that point, you'll give your fifteen-second elevator pitch, custom-made for your prospect's segment, industry, organization, and role. Then you'll ask casually, "I know you work for a large organization, and you've only been there for a short time. That said do you know if your organization is even interested in energy efficiency initiatives?"

It's highly likely your conversation partner will have no idea, which is fine, provided that you handle your follow-up questions properly. You might add, "I'm wondering who over there at your shop might be interested in energy efficiency initiatives. Do you happen to know who that might be?" You may be shocked to hear that the in-house energy guru sits only a couple of cubicles away from this newly hired exec. Or perhaps you'll hear, "I don't know, but I think it's Joe Smith… I probably have his email address in my phone… and even if I don't, you could certainly guess his email address—everyone at our company uses the same protocol: first initial and the first five letters of the last name, and then '@BigCompany. com.'"

If you're lucky enough to hear that your conversation partner sees your ultimate target on a regular basis, you might say, "Wow, what a small world! You know, you would be doing me the greatest personal favor if you were to give one of my cards to Mr. Smith when you see him next… In fact, here are two of my business cards, one for you and one for him. Would you be willing to hand-carry this card to him?" (I have never had someone refuse to do this favor for me. In most cases, the "messenger" places my business card in my target's hand the very next day.)

Always be sure to take your new friend's card because even if he's an "under-the-radar" staffer, it's great to drop his name when you connect with the person whose contact information you were given. When you reach out to your target, you might start with, "I met a very helpful young man named Brandon at the XYZ conference last Friday. I understand he just started working in your Chicago office. When I asked him who in your organization was responsible for energy-related projects, he was kind enough to volunteer your name and suggested that I reach out to you."

You never know who may be holding a key that can open a door of opportunity for you. Talk to people as human beings, not networking pawns. Genuinely network. Make those connections. And remember, the most useful chains usually have far more than two links in them!

GET YOURSELF A SEAT AT THE TABLE

Have you ever been in a situation where a prospect tells you that they need to talk to the rest of their committee before making any decisions? Committees are notorious for vetoing or tabling projects, so you should be ready to address the situation up front.

Unless you've prepared your prospect to give a stellar presentation and to fight for the project on your mutual behalf, there will be nobody at the committee meeting to address questions, objections, or misunderstandings. This puts your proposal at a high risk of being rejected.

Wouldn't it be a lot better if you could be in the room during the meeting? After all, you're the expert, and you're best equipped to not only explain

the benefits of your offering, but also field any questions or comments that may arise.

In my experience, people don't want vendors to attend internal meetings because they are afraid they'll monopolize the meeting and/or overhear confidential information. Here's an example of a conversation you might have with your prospect to get them to agree to let you sit in on the meeting:

PROSPECT: "I've got to take this to the committee."

YOU: "I understand. When does the committee meet?"

PROSPECT: "Every Thursday."

YOU: "How long is your typical committee meeting?"

PROSPECT: "About an hour."

YOU: "How many topics are typically discussed at the meeting?"

PROSPECT: "About a half a dozen."

YOU: "Okay, so if everyone gets to the meeting on time, you've got an hour to talk about six topics. That's an average of ten minutes per topic. Am I correct?"

PROSPECT: "Yes, that's right."

YOU: "What do you think the chances are of my attending that meeting?"

PROSPECT: "Hmmm… I don't think vendors are allowed to attend our committee meetings."

YOU: "Well, let me be frank. Do you think there's anybody in the world who is more capable of addressing questions on this project than I am? If you want to get your project approved [notice I say "your" instead of "my" to get the prospect more emotionally invested in seeing the project approved], the best thing you can do is get me in that room. And I'll make a deal with you: If you have ten minutes for each topic, you get me in the room at whatever point in the agenda you want me there. Invite me into the room just for that agenda item, and I'll leave immediately after presenting our proposal and fielding questions. I will not exceed my allotted time, and I will not be present during any confidential discussions. In other words, I can sit in the lobby, you can bring me in at minute twenty, and I will be out of there at minute thirty, graciously thanking you for inviting me to join the meeting. After I leave, you folks can continue with your other agenda items. I can assure you that in three or four minutes, I can make a compelling case to make sure you get your project approved, and in the next four to six minutes, I can answer any questions that come up in the wake of that little presentation. Frankly, if you had me in the room, I think you'd have a greater chance of getting your project approved."

If you put these types of parameters around your requested participation, you might actually get invited to "sing for your supper" at that meeting, and you'll have an excellent chance of emerging from that meeting with everyone else primed to say "yes" when the vote to approve the project is taken after you leave the room.

Keep in mind that even with the above-referenced impassioned plea to be invited to the meeting, some killjoy on the committee may still veto your participation. So what to do?

Let's be realistic. In most cases, the decision to approve your project will be made in a room you've never entered, by folks you've never met, at a time you're unaware of. The only way to prevail in circumstances such as these is to arm your internal champion with a compelling proposal that will stand on its own without you in the room. What does that mean? It means you have to equip your internal champion with a compelling and memorable fifteen-second elevator pitch. You have to give him a one-page proposal in unlocked PDF format so that he can liberally "borrow from it" to insert your ideas into his management brief or capital request. You have to also provide a one-page financial analysis that is both transparent

and compelling. I like to say that (with the exception of the spoken elevator pitch), you should be able to give your materials to the world-famous mime Marcel Marceau and see your project approved behind closed doors!

I heard a story the other day about a national sales manager for a large HVAC vendor in the Midwest who had done just that. He had given a California-based contractor an elevator pitch, a one-page proposal, and a one-page financial analysis using the skills he had acquired at one of our weeklong Efficiency Sales Professional™ Boot Camps. Sure enough, the contractor was able to carry those expertly crafted tools to his customer and close a $500,000 HVAC project using the Midwest vendor's equipment.

"If the success or failure of this planet and of human beings depended on how I am and what I do, how would I be and what would I do?"

BUCKMINSTER FULLER

WORK FOR OTHERS AND LET OTHERS WORK FOR YOU

There are not enough hours in the day to find every potential customer the old-fashioned way. Taking the time to locate and forge partnerships with non-competitive vendors or service providers is one of the best ways to maximize your time in finding new prospects. Here's an example that illustrates the point perfectly:

A company that sells bottled water to office buildings and an interior commercial plant maintenance vendor were both trying to find new leads and increase sales. Neither one of them was really fond of getting thrown

out of buildings that had "No Soliciting" signs on them, but they both knew that they had to grow their respective businesses.

One day, the plant vendor said to the water vendor, "You know what? When you deliver water to your current customers, what do you do? You walk from the front of your customer's office suite all the way back to the staff kitchen to deliver the full bottles and cart away the empties. The next time you make your deliveries, maybe you could do me a favor and take the long way in each suite, looking left and right as you pass through. See if they have any plants at all and, if they do, notice if they're fancy plants or plain ones—and notice how healthy they look. Oh, and when you drop off your invoice with the office manager, ask him if they take care of their plants themselves or if they outsource the work. Do you think you could do that for me?"

Excited by the potential to get the inside scoop on dozens of office suites he had never visited, the plant vendor continued with his part of the deal. "By the way, whenever I go into my clients' offices, the first place I have to go is to the kitchen sink to get water for their plants. While I'm there, I'll look around the kitchen to see whether or not they have bottled water. If they do, I'll make note of what size bottle they buy—whether it's those big round ones or the neat, square, stacking ones. Then, I'll see how many full and empty bottles they have on hand. That should give you a good idea of how much water they buy each month, right?"

The arrangement made so much sense, the pact was sealed on the spot. The plant and water vendors agreed to do a little research and give each other data on their customers' needs for each other's products… and the name and number of each office manager to boot!

As you might imagine, their sales skyrocketed as a result. There was no more sneaking past security guards… No more knocking on strange doors… No more ignoring "No Soliciting" signs. They were both already behind enemy lines. They just needed to share easy-to-collect data that could be leveraged to grow their respective revenues.

Now, how does this apply to energy efficiency? If you're in the HVAC business, you should be partnering with a lighting vendor. You should say, "Give me a list of twelve questions I can ask while I'm onsite doing my HVAC improvements so I can tell whether or not this might be a good prospect for a lighting upgrade. I don't have to know everything there is about illuminating engineering; I just need to know the twelve questions you would ask to determine if it's a worthwhile prospect for you to pursue. In return, I will give you my list of twelve questions. Every time you're doing a lighting audit, you can ask the chief engineer my list of questions and send the answers back to me. If I score it and they become a legitimate prospect, I'll follow up with them. We could give each other referral fees for deals that actually close, or just monitor the flow of leads back and forth to make sure the sharing is mutually beneficial."

That's a great way to get cross-promotion, very informally. Your non-competitive colleagues are in buildings all day long. Why are you not having them carry your questionnaire in there, taking five minutes with the chief engineer? It would have taken you five hours to get a meeting; however, your partner is already there. Have your collaborator ask the questions that you need to have answered in order to determine if his client represents a good prospect for your offerings. If the answer is "yes," then act on it immediately. And if you close the sale, be sure to thank your collaborator! You now owe him a debt of gratitude!

By the way, don't wait for your collaborator to score you a hot lead to put effort into trying to score one for him! Have your people carry his questionnaire to your job sites. It's quite rewarding to help a colleague close a sale. And the psychic debt that such a sale evokes is a wonderful incentive for your collaborator to redouble his efforts to do the same thing for you.

WHAT ARE YOU WAITING FOR?

Technology is constantly improving, and when you're trying to sell efficiency, you'll inevitably encounter prospects who want to wait for "the next big thing" or for production costs to decrease before they're willing to buy. So how do you overcome this objection? Show your prospect the cost of delay. In many cases, you can pay for the current generation of technology through savings long before the new one becomes available.

A few years ago, I met a utility-scale solar installation developer who we'll call Tom. He told me that he was tired of hearing his prospects say, "I'm going to wait on this project because the cost of silicon is going down, and the panels will likely be 50 percent cheaper in five years."

What did he do about this situation? He said, "I finally decided to put an Excel spreadsheet together to prove that the cost of the panels is only 20 percent of the job. Copper, framework, labor, and all that other stuff is the other 80 percent of the cost. And all of those things are going *up* in price rather than down."

So even if the protesting prospect turned out to be right and the cost of the panels dropped by 50 percent in five years, the price of 80 percent of the job was going *up* by 3 percent a year, compounded annually. On top of that, if the prospect decided to wait five years, he would lose five years' worth of potential solar energy production.

Tom said that as soon as he started showing off that spreadsheet, his prospects had little difficulty understanding that waiting for the price of silicon to go down was foolhardy.

Don't let prospects wait to buy. Make the effort to quantify the cost of delay and share it with them. Let the figures do the selling for you.

"If you do the right thing all the time, sooner or later you'll do it at the right time."
MARSHALL LEVIN

CROSS-SELLING AND UPSELLING

Cross-selling and upselling are two great ways to increase revenue, add value for your customers and, in some circumstances, form partnerships with non-competitive vendors and service providers.

Cross-selling: Adding an additional product or service to the sale that ideally not only increases your revenue, but also creates added value for your customer. In some cases, this involves partnering with a non-competitive vendor or service provider to deliver a valuable service that you don't offer. If you're selling LED lighting, for example, and the customer says, "I need the LED lighting retrofit, but I'd also like a better way to know which lighting is energized at any given time," you could say, "Well, we don't carry lighting controls. However, we do have an excellent source that we've used successfully for other projects. In fact, we could bundle the whole thing—my lights and their controls—in the same contract."

Now you can bring new business to a non-competitive partner *and* add value for your customer while saving him the headache of sourcing and hiring another vendor.

Upselling: Selling more expensive products or services that the customer did not originally intend to buy. The goal of upselling, of course, is to increase the income earned from the transaction, ideally while delivering a more complete solution for your client. In many cases, you'll end up with a more satisfied customer because (assuming your products and services are priced fairly) the added value will be more than worth the extra cost. Here's an example of upselling that is a variation of the example above:

Your customer, the landlord of an office building with fifty tenants, calls you and is interested in upgrading to an LED lighting system. After asking a series of targeted questions, you realize that the subject property is located in a demand-response-sensitive utility territory *and* that the lease form used by this landlord permits him to charge $25 per hour for after-hours lighting—provided he can track each tenant's extra hours of use!

You recommend a more sophisticated lighting system than the customer was initially requesting. Your solution would allow the building to dim its lighting during critical peak pricing periods for electricity *and* track each tenant's lighting usage, producing a report that would facilitate tenant billing for those allowable after-hours charges at the end of each month.

Without a doubt, the system you are recommending is both more sophisticated and more expensive than what the customer had in mind when he first contacted you. However, it may be easy to justify the incremental cost given the powerful advantages provided by the better system.

HYPOTHESIS-BASED SELLING

You first learned to hypothesize, or make educated guesses, in grade school science class. Now it's time to reframe that blast from the classroom past as a business tool.

In hypothesis-based selling, the method championed in the breakaway bestseller *The Challenger Sale*, one's ability to predict the needs of a prospect's organization is a critical component to success.

A hypothesis-based seller leads with ideas about what his prospect's organization needs. To put this method into practice, you need to do some homework. Research the organization's industry and history so that you enter the initial meeting with several hypotheses on your prospect's challenges—in other words, your ideas on their needs. Focus on big-picture outcomes rather than measurements or technical details at this stage.

Next, reframe your hypotheses in the context of a bigger problem or opportunity. Your unique insights into your prospect's challenges become your unique value in the eyes of that prospect.

Hypothesis-based selling works because you are giving the prospect a new opportunity rather than focusing on a known problem. Don't ask a prospect what he or she needs and then explain how you will fulfill that need. Tell your prospect what he or she needs and then explain the unique value you bring to the opportunity.

"If you are not continually learning and upgrading your skills, somewhere, someone else is. And when you meet that person, you will lose."
REID BUCKLEY

MAKE THE CARDS COUNT

Think back to the last networking event you attended. If you were focused on the job at hand, you probably left with at least a couple dozen business cards of people you met at the event. Unless you have a super-human memory, it's unlikely that you'll be able to remember details about every person with whom you exchanged cards.

So how do you make the business cards count? As soon as you turn away from the person, write three pieces of information on the back of his or her card before you stow it away:

- Where you met.
- What you talked about, particularly anything funny or otherwise memorable (this can be used when you follow up with the person).
- What the next step is.

In my experience, most people don't take the time to write these detailed notes, so be sure to jog their memory using your notes when you follow up with them.

One great technique that my wife uses for making sure people remember her is to present *two* of her cards. She will hand someone two cards and say, "Here's my card… and here's an extra one in case you lose the first one." That comment inevitably evokes a chuckle from the prospect. More importantly, when her new acquaintance goes through the stack of cards he collected during the event, she will be the only person with *two* cards in the pile. It's memorable and distinguishes you from the rest of the pack (pun intended).

"Ability is what you're capable of doing.
Motivation determines what you do.
Attitude determines how well you do it."
LOU HOLTZ

WHAT'S THE URGENCY?

Conveying the cost of delay is a well-worn sales technique. You can use rebate program expiration dates and other time-sensitive, cost-saving measures to your advantage. You have to be careful about selling on fear of price increases, though, because that can come off as high-pressure selling. Of course, if there are legitimate time constraints related to price, it's appropriate to emphasize the value of acting quickly.

Sometimes the importance of acting swiftly is very impressive. Other times, it's not. A few years ago, I was given a proposal to critique for a $300,000 lighting retrofit. The energy services company had used a standard report template that showed how much energy would be saved in kilowatts and kilowatt-hours, and which rebates the prospect was qualified to receive. The proposal also showed the carbon footprint reduction in terms of the equivalent number of cars that would be removed from area roadways by completing the retrofit.

In some circles, facts and figures like these have the potential to motivate swift action. In this case, however, the salesperson failed to check the self-calculating Excel spreadsheet before printing it. The report said that if the prospect invested $300,000 in this project, it would be the greenhouse gas equivalent of removing *0.94 cars* from area roadways.

You can just imagine what a jaded CFO might say after hearing, "I want you to spend $300,000 in return for knowing that you removed the equivalent of 0.94 cars from area roadways." You might hear something as genuinely sardonic as, "How about this? How about the board skips the lighting retrofit and gives *me* $100,000 instead. I promise to buy an all-electric Tesla with the money and lock my gas-guzzling sedan in my garage. That way, we'll remove the emissions of one *whole* car from area roadways instead of just 94 percent of a car, and our company can keep the other $200,000 in the corporate treasury! How about that?"

I use this example to show that you have to be careful whenever you're conveying the urgency of acting now. Make sure that your facts are compelling enough to merit the risk that you take of coming off as a pushy salesperson who just wants to close the sale as quickly as possible.

"He who is the most flexible will always prevail."
MARK T. JEWELL

A NETWORKING STORY

What do you do when you meet someone at a networking event who works in an entirely different industry than the one in which you're prospecting? I'm sure many of us would be inclined to say, "Nice to meet you…" and immediately move on to someone more relevant. If you find yourself in this situation, don't walk away. Here's a story that demonstrates the value of making connections outside of your own industry:

Not too long ago I met a colleague for lunch, and he looked very downtrodden. I said, "Hey, what's going on?" He said, "Last night I went to this trade org event. I just wasted my time." I said, "What are you talking about? You're usually so upbeat, and that audience is full of prospects for you." He continued with exasperation, "I spent twenty minutes pitching to a guy and then I asked, 'What do you do?' and he said, 'I sell rugs.' I wasted twenty minutes of my networking time talking to a guy who sells *rugs*!"

There are two aspects of this story worth noting. First, if you knew ahead of time that this person sold carpet, would you have used a different elevator pitch and/or spent a different amount of your valuable networking time? Second, what might that new and improved elevator pitch have sounded like? Here's one way the interaction *could* have gone:

"Hey, how are you doing? I'm John."
"I'm Bill."
"Hello, Bill. So what brings you to this event tonight?"
"I work for XYZ Carpets."
"Oh, I guess you sell rugs."
"Yes. We do."
"Whom do you sell to?"
"Commercial offices, mostly."
"Aha. You know I sell to a lot of commercial office buildings as well. Who are some of your favorite clients around town?"
"Equity Office… and Boston Properties."
"So I bet you do work for Tom at Embarcadero Four?"
"Oh yeah. We helped him with several tenant fit-outs last year. He's a great guy."
"Wow, Tom's a great guy. I've known him for years. Who else do you sell to? I bet we sell to a lot of the same folks…"

Before long, you'll be exchanging business cards and perhaps even working out a deal to swap leads, cross-promoting each other's services. Now *that's* how it's supposed to work.

LOOKING BEYOND THE "GREEN AGENDA"

You can save a lot of time searching for new prospects for your efficiency offerings by targeting businesses that have a "green agenda." In order to do this successfully, though, you need to take a closer look at what their green agenda actually entails.

Many companies will put up the façade of being "green" without really investing time and money into genuinely green measures. Some of these companies will run sexy press releases about what they're *going* to do rather than what they've actually done. Others will take the liberty of calling themselves "green" by investing in low-cost measures like compost bins or recycled paper or eco-friendly kitchenware.

The companies you should be targeting need to have the capital to invest in real efficiency measures as well as a demonstrated desire to act on their "green" intentions. Ideally, these prospects will have actually followed through on at least one efficiency-related project of some significance.

A "green agenda" may be a sign of a promising prospect. However, you must dig deeper. Make sure that agenda is more than just a façade and that the prospect is actually worth pursuing.

"Have the courage to follow your heart and intuition.
They somehow already know what you truly want to become."
STEVE JOBS

THREE-SENTENCE PROSPECTING

Assuming you have a strong understanding of who your key customers are and which customer profiles you're most interested in pursuing, what's the most efficient way to capture the attention of new prospects?

I have found the "three-sentence email" to be a great tool for opening conversations with new prospects quickly and effectively. Here's how it works:

Analyze your list of customers and separate it into groups based on building type, building size, building age, and any other relevant factors that define your ideal target(s). Then, search for buildings that have similar attributes. Once you've made a list of potential buildings to target, send each a "three-sentence email" similar to the following, which has been customized to target a potential common area lighting upgrade:

1. As you may have noticed, we recently upgraded the common area lighting in the Citibank Building at 100 Main Street, improving the lighting levels by 20 percent while reducing the energy use by more than 40 percent.
2. It occurred to me the other day as I passed your ground floor lobby that you are currently using the same lighting technology that we replaced at 100 Main Street.
3. If you would be interested in exploring how we could extend the success we delivered for 100 Main Street to your building, I'd be open to a conversation.

It's as simple as that. There are several things to note about this very streamlined and highly effective prospecting email:

- Offering a noteworthy project and specific savings statistics demonstrates that this is not your first rodeo. (Please also note that the increase in lighting levels was mentioned before energy savings, realizing that most building managers are more concerned with curb appeal than energy efficiency when it comes to their main lobbies.)
- Highlighting a successful case study within a block or two of your prospect's building makes it more real. He may know the owner/manager of the building you cited. He may even pass the building on his way to/from work, which will remind him to reply to your email if he hasn't already done so.
- Using the word "exploring" in the final sentence suggests a very low-pressure first meeting. It implies that you don't know whether your services would be appropriate or not; however, you're willing to explore the possibilities with your prospect.

- Saying "I'd be open to a conversation" also subliminally reinforces that this is not going to be a high-pressure sales call. The wording is almost coy in tone, which is a good thing as you position yourself as an expert who agrees to meet with potential clients at their urging, but does not force the issue if they're not genuinely interested at the end of the day.

Handled properly, this solicitation style will yield amazing results. You can use this same three-sentence approach when cold calling as well.

"Happiness is not something you postpone for the future;
it is something you design for the present."
JIM ROHN

YOU'RE THE CONNECTION

The more you think of yourself as the connection between a product or service that is available and someone who needs it, the more effective a sales professional you'll be. This shift in perspective can have an enormous impact on your performance across the board.

A recent attendee at our Efficiency Sales Professional™ Boot Camp recommended a book called *The Psychology of Sales Call Reluctance* by George W. Dudley and Shannon L. Goodson. It's quite a thick tome. My first reaction upon seeing the book was that someone could delay making cold calls for a *very long time* if he elected to read it cover to cover rather than just picking up the phone!

It's been said that one of the easiest to visualize and most helpful tricks for overcoming cold call reluctance is to imagine that you're calling your prospect to return his or her wallet, which we'll assume you found in the back of a taxicab.

Why is this little thought experiment so helpful? Because if properly visualized, it will have a dramatic effect on the way you're going to address the person who answers your call. For one thing, the gatekeeper is not going to prequalify you with twenty questions if it appears you are calling to *give* rather than take, and the way you communicate while you're in this mental "zone" will definitely give the impression that you have something important and valuable to offer.

Staying with this scenario for another moment, how much do you think that hypothetical lost wallet is really worth? Let's assume your prospect is well-heeled and has great taste in leather goods. Say it's a TUMI wallet lined with a couple hundred dollars of cash your prospect had just withdrawn from the ATM. It also holds a few high-limit credit cards, a driver's license, and perhaps some other items that are relatively easy to cancel or replace. The whole value of the "prize"? Probably less than $500, including the labor cost of his assistant who would wind up replacing the wallet and reporting the credit cards lost.

Now, let's return to the *real* reason for your call—an expense-reducing capital project with a projected life of a decade or more. What is the net present value (NPV) of the energy-saving solution you're about to introduce to this prospect? Is it $500? How about $5,000? How about $50,000? If you're selling complex solutions, the NPV might well exceed *half-a-million* dollars! Think about it—That's equivalent to returning *one thousand lost wallets* worth $500 apiece! *Now why would you ever hesitate to pick up the phone to return a thousand wallets?*

Don't ask yourself, "Why would this guy want to take my phone call?" You should be asking instead, "Why in the world would this person *not* want to take my phone call? It's as if I found a thousand of his wallets in the back of a taxicab and am calling to return them!"

Regardless of which mind game you deploy to overcome cold call reluctance, always remember one thing: You have something valuable to offer, and *you* are the connection that links your prospect to that value.

"No artist is ahead of his time. He is his time.
It is just that the others are behind the time."
MARTHA GRAHAM

WHY THE FREE AUDIT DOESN'T WORK

Many efficiency businesses offer free audits as a thin edge of the wedge to open conversations with new prospects. Free audits seem great in theory, but in practice, they don't work for at least a couple of reasons:

- If the customer doesn't have enough money to pay for an audit, he or she is not likely to have enough money to pay for your other services.
- Free audits are very easy to approve—who would say no to that? The problem is that in many cases, the person approving the audit doesn't talk to the real decision-makers before accepting the free

audit because there is no money involved in the transaction. If the prospect doesn't have to ask for even $500 to pay for the audit, it means you've never gotten his or her manager's approval to do the audit (which means that you don't necessarily have that manager's approval to do *any* improvements that come out of the audit). Are you really going to dedicate all this time and money to do an audit and not even have the buy-in of your prospect's boss?

On a related note, there is added benefit in getting yourself into the payable system of the organization from the very start. This makes your prospect less inclined to take your audit and then hire someone else to do the job because they already went through the effort of adding you to the system.

Assuming you agree that the free audit is fraught with peril, what might you offer a prospect instead? I recommend that you seriously consider offering free ENERGY STAR® benchmarking exercises. There are several benefits to using this approach to get your foot in the door:

- It takes a lot less time to benchmark a building using the EPA's ENERGY STAR® Portfolio Manager® software than to audit it.
- The report is automatically produced by the benchmarking tool, saving you countless hours preparing your audit report.
- Your prospect can't "shop" your benchmarking report, a common problem you run into as unscrupulous prospects simply hand your document to their incumbent contractor, relative, or friend to see how inexpensively they could do the work without your involvement.
- The Portfolio Manager® offers a 1-100 rating on nearly two dozen space types, and buildings that receive a rating of 75 or higher can qualify for the prestigious ENERGY STAR® label.

- If your benchmarking report winds up finding the building to be ENERGY STAR® label-worthy, you've created an "award" that the building owner didn't even know about until you arrived on the scene. That generates "psychic debt" in your favor.
- If the score proves that the building owner was overly sanguine about his building's present level of efficiency, you can dispel the complacency using an authoritative, unbiased, governmental source to break the news to your prospect that the building needs your help.
- Assuming you secure some retrofit work in the wake of doing the initial benchmarking exercise, you can continue to use Portfolio Manager to track the building's efficiency gains on a normalized basis. That means that even if the utility bill goes up in the wake of your retrofit, you can prove that it was perhaps due to a change in use (e.g., additional data center space) or a change in the cost per kilowatt-hour of electricity, rather than your retrofit failing to deliver the efficiency gains that you promised. Many decision-makers reluctantly approve capital for efficiency-related upgrades, hoping to see some evidence that they made the right decision prior to authorizing additional dollars for further efficiency initiatives. Seeing the ENERGY STAR® Portfolio Manager® score jump in the wake of a retrofit provides evidence that can be leveraged to build confidence for additional retrofit activity.

"Never mistake motion for action."
ERNEST HEMINGWAY

REFRAMING THE REFRIGERATOR

Suppose your goal is to convince the landlord of a multifamily property to improve the energy efficiency of his building by replacing the kitchen appliances in his apartments. You may very well find that he doesn't give a hoot about appliance efficiency, since his tenants are the ones paying the utility bills. This is an all-too-common scenario. Some people call it the "split incentive" problem. Guess what? You have a much greater chance of commanding your prospect's attention—and prevailing at the end of the day—if you reframe your value proposition with the help of some segment-specific business acumen.

Let's return to the example of the landlord whose apartment building is filled with old appliances. Your job is to convince him to replace those appliances with ENERGY STAR®-labeled ones. What are the benefits? New appliances require less maintenance, which means fewer disruptions for tenants and fewer headaches for the landlord, right? Since they're new, they're also more aesthetically pleasing, which should help with tenant retention and attraction, right? And, of course, they result in lower utility bills—admittedly a benefit the tenants reap if the building is submetered.

If you present these facts exactly the way I just did to a skeptical landlord, you'll probably fail to close the sale. Why? The investment of time and money is not worth a few less maintenance calls and an ambiguous increase in tenant attraction or retention. So how do you reframe this scenario to hit the ball out of the park? *Take the time to quantify and monetize the benefits of replacing these appliances using terminology that is sure to resonate with the landlord.*

I was advising a large public benefits program last year on how they could increase the market penetration of their multifamily direct-install programs. I suggested they determine the approximate difference in utility bills between an apartment outfitted with ENERGY STAR®-labeled appliances and one that is not. They did the math, and I believe it turned out to be about $40 a month in utility savings for a one-bedroom apartment.

Knowing this information, your pitch to the landlord could go something like this: "What if you invested roughly $1,000 to install ENERGY STAR®-labeled appliances in each of your units and then you said to every prospective tenant, 'These newly installed appliances will lower your utility bill by about $40 per month. You may have noticed that our rent is about $20 per month higher than the building across the street; however, with a utility bill that is $40 lower per month, you'll wind up keeping an extra $20 in your pocket every month that you can use to buy a six-pack of your favorite craft beer.'" (I was told that beer was the most fungible currency among young renters in that particular town. Feel free to modify this pitch to appeal to your local audience.)

The next step is quantifying and monetizing the landlord's share of the benefits. What does an incremental $20 per month in rent mean to the apartment building's profitability and value? $20 per month equals $240 per year. Using the Direct Capitalization Approach to appraisal and a capitalization rate of 10%, that incremental Net Operating Income of $240 per year has the potential to drive $2,400 worth of incremental asset value for the landlord! That's nearly 2.5 times the cost of the new appliances. Moreover, at a lower cap rate, the jump in appraised value would be even more pronounced. Keep in mind that the landlord wouldn't have to sell the building to enjoy the benefits of that bump in appraised value. It also increases the amount of equity he could take out when refinancing the building.

And by the way, what if the new appliances helped retain a tenant? The landlord benefits further by avoiding some or all of the following costs of tenant "churn":

* The leasing commission.
* Rent lost while seeking a replacement tenant.
* The cost of cleaning, repainting and potentially re-carpeting the unit, as well as the rent foregone while doing so.
* Rent lost during a "free-rent period" if such a perk is customary to induce a new tenant to sign.

After presenting such a compelling case, you should have the landlord's undivided attention. You've shown him the true value of the proposed project on the back of an envelope (or beer coaster as the case may be). Moreover, you've shown him how to reframe the upgrade for both his current and prospective tenants. His current tenants should willingly accept the installation inconvenience, and his new tenants should gladly accept slightly higher rent, in exchange for lower utility bills and the convenience and aesthetics of brand new ENERGY STAR®-labeled appliances.

"I am always doing that which I cannot do,
in order that I may learn how to do it."
PABLO PICASSO

BUT IT'S VACANT...

Have you ever tried to sell an efficiency product or service to a prospect who owns or manages a building with high vacancy? If you have, you probably know that it's not an easy task. Vacant space doesn't pay rent, and without that money, it can be hard to convince a prospect to front capital for efficiency improvements to those square feet. I'd like to share a success story from a graduate of the Efficiency Sales Professional™ Certificate program (who we'll call Tom) about his experience prevailing in such a situation.

Tom approached a developer in Silicon Valley who owned a building that was 35 percent vacant with the goal of selling him a high-end lighting control solution. The offering was a state-of-the-art system that allowed the user to control the brightness of each and every luminaire ("lighting fixture" in layman's terms) using a desktop widget that connected the user's computer to a server, which in turn was networked to the lighting ballasts, each of which had a unique IP address. It was a truly high-tech system, and its price reflected it—it would cost about $4 per square foot to install.

Tom approached the developer with the following elevator pitch: "You know, the kinds of tenants that you're hoping to attract are most likely high-tech prima donnas—venture capital-backed game designers and the like. They would really appreciate this technology." The developer asked him, "What are you getting at?" Tom replied confidently, "Well, your building is 35 percent vacant now. I suggest that you buy our high-tech lighting control system for the 35 percent of your building that is vacant so that you can use it as a differentiating amenity as your brokers try to find tenants to fill that space."

The developer thought about it for a few moments. He said, "If you're willing to sign a memorandum of understanding saying that you're not going to sell this system to any other building within twenty-five miles of mine (so that my brokers can actually use this lighting control system as a differentiating amenity), then I'll buy the system from you. Of course, you also have to agree to educate our brokers as to how special it actually is (and why it's important to our potential tenants' productivity, etc.) so they can effectively leverage this competitive advantage and fill up the building with rent-paying tenants."

Tom didn't consider the twenty-five mile radius limitation to be onerous, so he agreed, and they signed the deal.

What happened in the wake of the retrofit? Six months later, the building's vacancy percentage had dropped to 5 percent! Who do you

think made more money: Tom, who sold a $4-per-square-foot system, or the landlord, who just filled up 30 percent of his building? The landlord, of course! Think about the annual rent per square foot and the concomitant increase in appraised value that the landlord enjoyed now that his building was 95 percent occupied.

There's a funny epilogue to this story as well: After the tenants moved in, they called Tom and said, "Listen, we like the system, but we don't like the way it's programmed. Could we pay you to reprogram it for us?" Tom agreed, of course, and made another couple bucks per square foot reconfiguring the system. Within a six-month period, Tom closed two sales: one for $4 per square foot and the second one for $2!

Most salespeople would probably have approached this situation saying, "There's no way a landlord is going to spend money outfitting vacant space, especially not with a top-of-the-line lighting control system. Why would they buy from me?" Tom, a true sales professional, used the powers of positive thinking and reframing. He understood exactly what was most important to the landlord and reframed his offering based on that insight.

The more you can reframe energy efficiency as an *amenity that gets people more of what they already know they want* (in this case, more occupied square feet!), the more successful you'll be at selling it.

> *"Half-efforts do not produce half-results.*
> *They produce no results."*
> HARRY BECKWITH

WHICH DO YOU CHOOSE?

As a sales professional, you're constantly asking people to make choices. Depending on the complexity of the job, you may be asking your prospect to make dozens—even hundreds—of decisions. As we all know, making choices can be difficult, and the psychology of how people make choices is both fascinating and very relevant to our jobs as sales professionals.

Those of you who have attended the Efficiency Sales Professional™ Boot Camp know that I'm a big fan of TED Talks. One of my favorite TED Talks is called "The Art of Choosing" by Sheena Iyengar. This twenty-four minute presentation contains great insights about how to cut down the number of choices you present; how to concretize the choices so that people can visualize the outcome; how to categorize those choices to make choosing easier; and, how to condition for complexity to allow people to survive the arduous process of decision-making.

In her TED Talk, Sheena is quick to point out that most senior executives make more than a hundred decisions a week, with about half of them made in nine minutes or less. The typical salesperson will waste time debating whether it's worth the effort to spend several hours distilling the proposal into a single page. The sales professional realizes that if half of all decisions are made in nine minutes or less, it is vital to provide a document that can be read in less than four minutes, leaving the other five minutes to contemplate whether or not to take the action indicated on the last line of that carefully crafted one-pager.

Do yourself a favor and watch Sheena's TED Talk. I have gained several valuable insights from this presentation, and I think you will, too.

"Choice can develop into the very opposite of everything it represents in America when it is thrust upon those who are insufficiently prepared for it."

SHEENA IYENGAR

ARE YOU FOCUSING ON THE RIGHT BENEFITS?

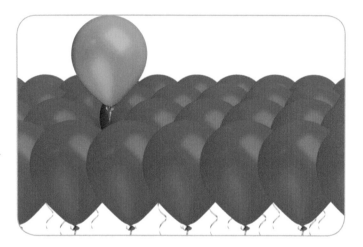

Suppose you are targeting a large building that you know has plans to do an efficiency upgrade. Chances are a lot of other salespeople are vying for the same job. So how do you set yourself apart from the competition? I can confidently say that most of your competitors are going to focus on the energy metrics (saved kilowatts, kilowatt-hours, therms, etc.) and the most obvious financial impacts—the cost of the project, the utility cost savings, and perhaps utility rebates or incentives.

Sure, people care about money, but utility-cost financial savings alone are often not compelling enough to motivate a major change to the built environment. You can set yourself apart by highlighting the non-utility-cost financial benefits (which are often an order-of-magnitude larger than the utility cost savings) as well as any non-financial benefits that are applicable.

What non-utility-cost financial benefits might you emphasize? That depends on how well you know the business dynamics of your prospect's market segment and individual role. How might your project produce benefits that can be quantified and monetized? How well can you reframe your project's benefits so that they can be measured with yardsticks your prospect is already using to gauge his/her success? Need some examples of non-utility-cost financial benefits to focus on? How about these for starters:

* Improvements in worker productivity.
* Improved occupant health.
* Reduced absenteeism or presenteeism.
* Improved attraction or retention of employees or tenants.

Realize that the above-referenced benefits are hardly hypothetical. There is plenty of empirical evidence supporting the connection between enhanced efficiency and every one of these benefits. These studies quantify and monetize the impacts in a wide variety of segments including office, healthcare, education, and more.

And by the way, once you've quantified and monetized the non-utility-cost financial benefits, remember to consider all the non-financial benefits as well—things like getting an ENERGY STAR® label, many of which actually wind up leaking value back into the non-utility-cost financial benefits bucket. As just one example, no less than a half-dozen recent studies have shown that ENERGY STAR®-labeled office buildings enjoy higher base rents, increased occupancy, and higher resale value. So

what you might have assumed to be a "feel-good" non-financial benefit may actually be a robust non-utility-cost financial benefit instead!

If you limit your conversation to utility-cost financial benefits or technical specs like kilowatts, kilowatt hours, and therms, get in line. *Every other vendor who has approached your prospect has talked about those same things.* When you talk about higher-order benefits—ones that are tailored to your prospect's segment, industry, organization, and role—you'll have a far more interesting and compelling interaction, and a much higher closing ratio to boot.

"A work is perfectly finished only when nothing can be added to it and nothing taken away."
JOSEPH JOUBERT

ARE YOU ASKING
THE RIGHT QUESTIONS?

In the words of Tony Robbins, "The quality of your life is directly related to the quality of the questions you ask."

So I ask you, are you asking the right questions?

Here is a list of some of my favorite questions to ask early in the conversation to make sure you are not wasting your time:

- Are there particular departments or individuals here that focus on energy efficiency?
- How many projects have been proposed here in the last "x" years?
- How many have been approved (and why)?
- What has prevented project approvals?
- Can you think of any previous efficiency initiatives that were particularly gratifying?
- What projects or initiatives are on your "wish list"?
- What percentage of your overhead is energy?
- How could energy efficiency boost productivity in your organization?
- What is the equivalent level of sales needed to equal $1 in energy cost reduction?
- How would upgrade costs and benefits be split between the landlord and the tenant(s)?
- How might the landlord's share of savings affect the building's profitability and value?
- What does your capital budgeting request process look like?

By the way, why do I use the word "gratifying" in one of the questions above? Because most decisions are made emotionally, and you need to find out exactly which emotions will motivate your prospect to take action.

"All progress takes place outside the comfort zone."
MICHAEL JOHN BOBAK

HOW CAN YOU CONNECT THE DOTS FOR A SMALL-BUSINESS OWNER?

If you want to tap into this "hard-to-reach" segment, you first need to ask yourself, "What are the priorities of a small-business owner?" With energy costs being a small fraction of their overall business expenses, leading into the conversation wearing your "saving energy" hat might not capture their attention.

As it turns out, years of research into this area have yielded a fairly good understanding of the small-business needs hierarchy. Studies have shown that most small-business owners care about these factors in the following order:

- Health and safety requirements
- Regulatory compliance
- Corporate improvement initiatives
- Maintenance
- Productivity

One survey of small-business concerns came up with this list of non-utility bill benefits that might resonate with small- and medium-sized business owners.

- Improved employee productivity
- Optimized operations
- Regulatory compliance
- Strategic maintenance planning
- Reliability and reduced downtime
- Public relations and shareholder value

So, you might ask, where does energy efficiency fit into either of these hierarchies? You need to connect the dots between your project and specific elements on their needs hierarchy in order to increase the likelihood of approval. It is possible for an energy-efficiency upgrade—even one that is very cost-effective (even direct install!)—to languish unapproved because some other alternatives are more attractive on some dimension other than cost-effectiveness.

"Clear your mind of can't."
SOLON

HELPING SMALL BUSINESSES VISUALIZE SAVINGS

What does a small-business owner care about? Most are running lean on working capital, so their primary concern is probably making payroll. This can be an issue if you're trying to sell efficiency products or services. The minute you start talking about the upfront cost of the project, the prospect's interest may wane.

Even if you offer a one-year payback, small-business prospects may still have to pass because their cash flow is already committed to keeping their doors open. Many simply don't have the cash to advance an entire year's utility savings today to pay for that one-year payback measure. Small-

business owners have to watch every dollar to ensure they stay viable. If you put yourself in their shoes, you could easily understand why. After all, what good is energy-efficient lighting if you can't make payroll?

So let's assume you're trying to sell a lighting retrofit for a small café that would produce a few thousand dollars in utility savings annually. How could you convince the owner that the efficiency investment is worth undertaking?

The most direct path to a "yes" could be helping the proprietor focus on the positive outcome rather than the first cost. You might ask, "If you had a few thousand dollars of extra working capital in your hands today, what would you do with it?" Then zip it. Just allow the question to hang in the air to give your prospect the time to consider it carefully before answering. He might say, "The first thing I'd do is replace our espresso machine that just died so we could once again sell coffee drinks at $4 a pop instead of the $2 we're now charging for drip coffee!"

You might respond, "That certainly makes sense. What if we could get creative about financing that lighting upgrade we've been discussing? What if we could secure a utility rebate for 50 percent of the project cost and six months of low-interest financing to cover the balance? I've already run the numbers, and the project's savings would fully amortize the 50 percent non-rebated portion in just six months. After that, all of your utility savings could go directly into a special account that you could eventually use to buy your new espresso machine with *cash*. Think about it. Before long, you could have both the lighting retrofit and the new espresso machine paid off. Your shop would look better than ever, you would be back in the $4-per-serving coffee business, and you would continue to enjoy lower utility bills for years to come."

WINE, CHEESE, AND LEDS

They say repetition is the mother of learning. You've heard me say more than once that one of the most valuable traits of an efficiency sales professional is the ability to *reframe efficiency so that it can be measured with yardsticks that the prospect is already using to measure his or her own success.* Here's a great example of someone doing exactly that:

One of our Efficiency Sales Professional™ Boot Camp graduates was trying to come up with a way to convince small retailers to invest in LED lighting retrofits. Before presenting the business owners with a compelling case about why the lighting retrofit would be a smart investment, she first asked herself, "What do these owners really care about?" She quickly realized, of course, that small retailers are very interested in increasing

foot traffic. After all, getting more customers to set foot in your store is the first step (pun intended) to boosting sales per square foot.

With this in mind, she came up with a creative campaign that would help *her* customers get more of *their* customers in their stores in the wake of a lighting upgrade. She targeted commercial areas that had concentrations of small retailers, walked into each of the stores and proposed the following offer: "If you and at least nine of your neighbors on this street sign up for a full lighting retrofit, my boss and I will sponsor a 'wine, cheese, and LEDs' party. We'll even bring sidewalk sandwich boards and little easels with signs on them proclaiming what a wonderful thing you and your neighbors did. We'll celebrate the fact that you're saving all this energy—and we'll drive traffic into your stores. Not only will this event make more potential customers aware of your establishments, but it will also let the world know that you are a socially conscious business."

The campaign was dramatically successful. Most people in this industry would agree that small businesses represent a hard-to-reach audience, fraught with high transaction cost, language barriers, and the like. However, the sooner you start talking about what *they* care about (foot traffic and incremental sales, rather than chromaticity, color rendering, simple payback period, and so forth), the easier it will be to capture their attention and retain it long enough to motivate them to take action.

I encourage you to ask yourself this simple question before you make your next sales call: "What does my prospect really care the most about?" The answer to that question will help you reframe your energy solutions so that they resonate with what your prospects are truly seeking.

EXPANDED LIFE-CYCLE
COST ANALYSIS

Too many of your prospects are fascinated with Simple Payback Period, and it makes *no* sense to focus on that metric in situations where you're comparing mutually exclusive solutions (i.e., situations where your prospect has two or more solutions to pick from, but at the end of the day they can only pick one). Keep in mind that when comparing two or more mutually exclusive choices, there are several dimensions you need to consider:

- What is the first cost of each alternative?
- How many years will each alternative likely last?

- What will it cost to operate and maintain each alternative for each year of its expected lifetime?

Provided that you do understand how your proposed solutions will create benefits beyond utility savings and service life, you might consider using an *expanded style of life-cycle cost analysis*. Are there any other benefits that should be factored in? Could those benefits be quantified? And, if so, would they result in secondary financial benefits that would wind up being much more important than the projected utility savings or even maintenance savings could ever be?

As an example, there was an office building in Canada whose HVAC equipment was so noisy that the last time they rented office space immediately adjacent to the building's core (where the equipment was located), pens would practically vibrate off the tenant's desk! Think of how much "secondary" financial benefit that landlord would receive if he could somehow quiet his mechanical systems and rent that marooned square footage! Doing so would allow the landlord to enjoy thousands of dollars of incremental net operating income, and ten times that much in incremental asset value using the income approach to appraisal (i.e., the direct capitalization approach) and a capitalization rate of 10 percent. In such a case, if you were doing a life-cycle cost analysis that compared the two scenarios—with and without the upgrade—you would be wise to consider the potential for incremental net operating income and asset value when calculating the financial advantages of doing the improvement.

In a conventional simple payback analysis, these valuation effects would not show up. Why? For two reasons:

- Most people focus only on first cost and utility savings when doing a simple payback period calculation.

◆ Even if they did broaden the analysis to include non-utility-cost financial benefits (e.g., the aforementioned incremental net operating income and subsequent increase in asset value), how much of that extra benefit would hit in the first year, which is the only year that the simple payback period analysis considers? Very little, if any. Therefore, even if these additional non-utility-cost financial benefits were on the decision-maker's radar, the simple payback period calculation would be blind to them.

As an epilogue to this story, I'm happy to report that the above-referenced Canadian landlord did, in fact, find a solution that effectively addressed his HVAC woes. The solution not only eliminated the noise and vibration that were preventing those orphaned square feet from being rented, but also produced energy savings as well. I subsequently heard that a successful pilot of this technology in one building gave the owner the confidence to install the same solution in sixteen additional properties.

Now *that's* an example of thinking outside the box, offering the prospect an energy-efficiency solution that addresses the central core (pun intended) problem and being rewarded handsomely when your carefully crafted solution is expanded to additional properties.

> *"Courage doesn't mean you don't get afraid.*
> *Courage means you don't let fear stop you."*
> BETHANY HAMILTON

HARNESSING EMOTIONS

Think about how you interact with your prospects. Are you going from the outside in, or are you going from the inside out? In my experience, most people go from the outside in. They just bombard people with information—technical cut sheets, charts, statistics, and so forth. "Here's all the data. What do you think?" And of course people are going to say (most often to themselves), "Good grief! I don't even know what to do with all of this information."

In most cases, purchasing decisions are *emotionally driven*. People are not always convinced by facts and figures. Think about what happens when you buy a car. Do they give you the boring, black and white, tissue-paper owner's manual and say, "Here, if you like the specs on this car, come in and see it."? When you buy a house, do they give you the technical specifications of the house—the construction drawings and the appliance specifications? Or do they work with you to help you build a connection with the house? Think about it. When real estate brokers take you around and show you the houses they think you'll like, do they show you the blueprints and appliance specs? Or do they show you the nicely manicured lawn and beautiful interior and then crow about how wonderful the schools are in the neighborhood?

I read a story the other day about a particularly successful new home developer who had a unique approach to getting his prospects to fall in love with his houses—before they were even built! He would literally take his prospects out to the site, where the "model home" was nothing more than a cement pad. He would then put a few chairs on the pad facing in the direction of the best view from that lot. He would invite the prospect(s) to sit down and imagine how good it would feel to be sitting in the living room and enjoying that view every night after a hard day at the office. How many prospects signed on the dotted line after that exercise in visualization? Let me put it this way: There's a reason he gained notoriety as being a particularly successful new home developer!

The same principle applies when selling efficiency, which for most folks is a wild and wooly intangible anyway. Your product or service needs to have an emotional appeal before you bring any technical discussion to the table. Focus on the "why" before you focus on the "what."

"Chase the vision, not the money;
the money will end up following you."
TONY HSIEH

MAKING IT REAL

They say a picture is worth a thousand words. Illustrating the stark contrast between "what is" and "what could be" is vital to your success in selling efficiency solutions. Moreover, taking the time to use illustration techniques that are creatively tuned to each prospect will definitely help you close more sales.

One of our Efficiency Sales Professional™ Boot Camp graduates (we'll call him John) recently showed me an energy upgrade proposal that he had done for the owner of a barbeque franchise in his hometown. This restaurateur didn't have a background in energy efficiency—he just knew how to run a successful eatery.

Realizing this, John decided to present a proposal that was almost entirely graphics, presented in the restaurant's trade dress colors and arranged on a single page. He even laminated it to mimic a restaurant menu! Projected savings were first converted to the cumulative profit the restaurant would enjoy from serving "x" number of incremental lunches per month. Those "virtual lunch equivalents" were then displayed as tiny line drawings of Styrofoam take-out boxes.

During his meeting with the owner, John simply pointed to that small army of boxes and said, "So which would you rather do? Approve the upgrade we've been talking about or find a way to start serving 'x' number of additional lunches each month?"

This is exactly the kind of lateral thinking that successful sales professionals employ every day to capture the attention of their prospects. If you have a prospect who would be overwhelmed by a proposal filled with technical and financial metrics, try using compelling visuals instead.

"Creativity is allowing yourself to make mistakes.
Art is knowing which ones to keep."
SCOTT ADAMS

WHEN DOES YOUR SALE END?

Many salespeople think that the sale ends when they collect their commission. Sales professionals are smart enough to know that extending the sales process to include a post-installation follow-up call yields tremendous benefits. Consider the following scenario:

> "Hi, Max. It's Mark with XYZ Lighting. I'm just giving you a courtesy call to follow up on the lighting upgrade we did at your facility in July. How do you like the new look?"
>
> "Hey, thanks for calling! Yep, the new lighting equipment is working out really well. No complaints at all."
>
> "Great to hear. Hey, while we're on the topic, I'd like to ask you a question that I make a point of asking all of my clients a few months

after installation. Are there any positive outcomes that you've noticed other than the ones we discussed when you decided to do the upgrade?"

"Funny you should ask… I was just chatting with our shop foreman last week; he told me that ever since those new lights were installed, our scrap rate has been down almost 10 percent. At first, he thought it was a fluke. Now that the system's been operating for almost three months, he's pretty sure the scrap reduction is here to stay. Frankly, I'm not surprised… His techs can finally see what they're cutting and drilling. Remember how dingy it was in the shop when you did your original lighting audit?"

"Wow, a 10 percent scrap rate reduction. Did your buddy happen to mention how significant the impact is in dollars and cents?"

"I was wondering the same thing, so I asked him. As crazy as it sounds, it's actually saving the company more money than the utility savings!"

"That's terrific. I bet your CFO will be happy to see the project throwing off twice as much return as he was expecting! Hey, do you mind if I use that little story you just shared when I speak with other small manufacturers with similar retrofit proposals?"

"Nope. Go right ahead. Just promise me that you're not going to sell any of those fancy new lights to our competitors! Unless, of course, you promise to charge them three times as much as we paid (chuckle)!"

Energy upgrades can generate three kinds of benefits: utility-cost savings (e.g., utility bill reductions, rebates, and incentives); non-utility-cost financial benefits (e.g., the above-referenced scrap reduction); and, non-financial benefits (e.g., getting an ENERGY STAR® label).

Most salespeople focus on the first and third buckets. Efficiency-focused sales professionals realize that the second bucket is often larger than the first! Moreover, they realize that the third bucket's benefits often spill over into the second bucket (e.g., ENERGY STAR®-labeled buildings evidencing higher rents, lower vacancy, and higher sales price).

The more you understand your segment (in this example, the impact of better lighting quality on scrap rates), and the more research you do *after the sale* to discover non-utility-cost financial benefits, the more comfortable you'll be emphasizing benefits beyond utility cost savings as you engage future prospects.

> *"Doing the best in this moment puts you in the best place for the next moment."*
> OPRAH WINFREY

REFRAMING COST SAVINGS

What do you do when your prospect fails to see the value of your product or service? Reframe it in a way that captures attention. There are many ways to do this, and some situations require a very creative approach to selling.

Here's a scenario courtesy of one of our recent Efficiency Sales Professional™ graduates and the creative solution we came up with to help him capture the attention of his prospect in a new and different way:

Mike (not his real name) was trying to sell an LED lighting retrofit to the owner of a couple dozen Southern California gas stations. He told me that his prospect was from out of the country, difficult to communicate with, and even more difficult to read. He was also somewhat elusive, which had already delayed lighting upgrades at these stations for many months. Mike knew the owner's favorite diner, which he was in the habit of visiting every Monday morning. This meant that there was at least *one* way to catch this character in person. Mike now needed to figure out how to get the owner's attention and convince him that this lighting retrofit—which had a net present value of $53,000—deserved an immediate approval and "notice to proceed."

Here's what we came up with: Mike would walk into the diner one Monday morning with a $53,000 unsigned check made payable to the gas station owner. He would ask to join him for coffee, and after a few minutes of casual conversation, remove the check from his pocket and slowly slide it across the table. "A check for $53,000? What is this for?" the gas station owner would ask. Mike would reply, "It's the net present value you'll enjoy by signing this purchase order and incentive application, the details of which I've already approved with the utility."

Now, Mike's prospect might not say "yes" immediately; however, I'd be surprised if this little stunt didn't get him thinking a lot more seriously about giving the long-awaited approval for this upgrade.

The moral of the story? Sometimes it pays to get visual. Sometimes it pays to understand what will really grab someone's attention. Sometimes you need to express the urgency in a new and different way. And to do that, it helps to be creative.

"Don't let your dreams be only dreams."
JACK JOHNSON

THE THREE R'S OF INFORMED SELLING

When you approach an organization with a proposed efficiency project, you have to be prepared to knock out the competition. You're competing with not only other energy solutions providers, but also non-efficiency-related projects that the organization might choose to fund instead. Here's a three-step process that will help you succeed:

1. **Read**: I'm always shocked at how few people subscribe to the trade journals and newsletters that cover their target customers' industries. If you're selling to supermarkets, you need to know everything that's going on in the grocery industry. What are the

latest trends? What types of investments are they making? What new technologies are grocery stores using? Keep yourself in the loop by reading the industry news so you can better predict what your prospects are likely to care about.

2. **Research**: In order to know how your products and services will benefit your prospect's organization, you need to find out everything you can about how that particular organization is structured and what they value. Maybe you'll discover that they frequently donate to charity, perhaps to publicize their commitment to the community. If so, you could emphasize the positive environmental impact of your efficiency project and suggest that you showcase that in a post-project press release.

3. **Reframe**: Industry and prospect-specific insights allow you to reframe your offering to resonate with the values and needs you've identified. So what are the most important things to talk about? What should you avoid discussing altogether? Write down any relevant information that you gather in the first two stages and come up with an informed sales strategy using that information.

"Don't let the fear of losing be greater
than the excitement of winning."
ROBERT KIYOSAKI

THE RIGHT METRICS

One of the major topics I cover at any of my financial analysis workshops is the importance of using proper rather than popular metrics when seeking project approvals. Your choice of financial metrics could determine whether a proposed project earns a thumbs-up or a thumbs-down.

Unfortunately, your prospects may be very attached to popular, substandard metrics like simple payback period, return on investment, and internal rate of return. In some cases, they may even be resistant to proper metrics like net present value, modified internal rate of return, or savings-to-investment ratio because they don't understand the calculations and would rather use what they already know.

When a prospect is using substandard metrics to drive capital budgeting decision-making—especially with expense-reducing capital projects—it's your job to be the adult in the relationship and to share with that person (in a "tough love" way if necessary) that those metrics are not going to serve them best.

Unless you know for a fact that your prospect is already using the right metrics to evaluate projects, it's a good idea to include both "popular" and "proper" metrics on your financial summary spreadsheet. This will allow you to compare the metrics they are used to seeing with the ones you recommend they start using, and through that comparison, demonstrate why they should be using more advanced metrics to evaluate the project.

"Education is not the filling of a pail,
but the lighting of a fire."
WILLIAM BUTLER YEATS

CONNECTING THE DOTS FOR A "HOT" PROSPECT

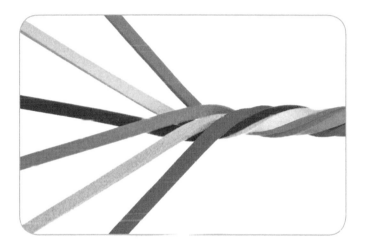

Before you meet with a decision-maker, you need to do some behind-the-scenes research. You need to dig up any and all information that will help you connect the dots for your prospect. The following scenario proves the point.

Jake (not his real name) was hoping to convince the owner of a local hotel to upgrade his air-conditioning system, which was well past its useful life, but still operating, thanks to a lot of unplanned maintenance and crossed fingers. The hotel in question was located in Central California, a place where temperatures soar in the summertime. Jake knew that the current

AC system was no longer able to maintain design temperature in the hot summer months—both the hotel's engineer and the front desk manager had shared that several guests had given them each an earful lately on how their rooms were hotter than they had bargained for.

The hotel was owned by an out-of-state investor who was so worried about the Central California economy that he had imposed a capital spending freeze on all of his assets there. Jake knew he needed to compile an inarguable case for upgrading the AC of this particular asset, something that would "shake the Etch-A-Sketch" for this owner and draw a new picture that would shake loose some capital.

So what did Jake do? He first paid a visit to the hotel's night auditor. Why the night auditor? Because he's the person who has firsthand knowledge of how many rooms they had rented in the preceding days, weeks, and months. He is also the person who knows in which direction the average daily room rate has been trending over time. He has a keen understanding of the hotel's break-even point. Bottom line: The night auditor was Jake's ticket to understanding the impact that AC-related declines in occupancy might be having on this hotel's income statement.

Jake explained to the night auditor, "Listen, I'm working with the owner to evaluate some potential capital improvements to this property, and a question popped into my mind the other day that I bet you could help me answer. Have you noticed any trends in occupancy in this hotel over the last six months?"

Much to Jake's satisfaction, the night auditor shared with him that occupancy had been consistently falling over the last several months; their monthly revenue was now nearly $40,000 lower than last year's monthly average. Jake then circled back with the front desk manager, a few local travel agents, and some other folks in the community. Guess what? The word on the street was that this hotel could no longer maintain design temperature in the hottest summer months. The locals now knew the property as "the hot hotel"—and by "hot hotel," they didn't mean the latest "must-visit" boutique property!

Shortly thereafter, Jake called the owner and laid out the facts. "You say you don't want to spend $250,000 upgrading your AC. Well, guess what? Over the last several months, you've actually been paying for the system you refuse to buy." When the owner replied, "What are you talking about?" Jake shared the results of his conversations with the night auditor, front desk manager, and others in the community. "Over the last six months, you've probably lost a quarter of a million dollars in room nights (which happens to be the entire cost of the AC system I recommended to you last month) because the word on the street is that you can't control the temperature during the summer months." He continued, "What do you think is going to happen when Hotels.com or Yelp picks up on the fact that your property is 'hot'—and not in the good sense? The locals already know it, which is why you're seeing fewer people referring their own visitors to your property. What happens the next time one of those "mystery shoppers" from Hotels.com dressed in a black leotard and white gloves drops in for a summer night's stay and you get dinged a couple stars because your rooms aren't cool enough? Your $40,000-a-month loss will get even larger. How low can your average occupancy sink before all those lost room nights put you below break-even? You could lose your hotel to the bank if this trend worsens."

As you might imagine, these carefully assembled data points, presented in such a compelling manner, finally captured the owner's attention. He would have been crazy not to take action when presented with the reality that the room nights his property had been losing represented more than the debt service on a brand new AC system.

It's all about having the insight and persistence to go behind the scenes and get tactical information that you can then communicate to the person who has the power to effect change. Even the most reluctant prospect can be turned into a buyer if you invest the time to research and connect the dots.

"I not only use all the brains that I have,
but all that I can borrow."

WOODROW WILSON

IF IT'S NOT ABOUT SAVING MONEY, WHAT IS IT ABOUT?

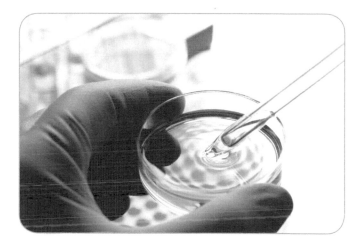

Whenever I do a national keynote speech or customized coaching session for a sales team, I make it a point to speak with several "rock stars" in the client's organization who are really knocking the ball out of the park. The highest performers always have offering-specific lessons that the rest of the sales team could learn for increasing their sales.

A large controls manufacturer recently asked me to present a general session keynote at its national sales meeting. As I was preparing my remarks, I had the pleasure of speaking with one of their rock stars. I asked him, "To what do you attribute your success selling controls in the laboratory segment?"

He replied that he specialized in controlling the energy used to power exhaust hoods in critical environments like labs, and that by doing so, he could reduce a facility's electricity use by more than half. In fact, he gave me an example of a lab for which he had reduced the bill by more than $350,000 per year.

I was certainly impressed. However, I was left wondering why a lab that was large enough to save that much electricity annually on its fume hoods—a lab that probably did several hundred million dollars of research a year—would take the time away from testing drugs or curing cancer to focus on something as obscure as fume hood fan energy savings—particularly when they'd have to interrupt their operations for several days to implement whatever savings maneuver this rock star ultimately proposed.

The rock star set me straight. He said, "You don't understand. When I propose a project that will save $350,000 a year, I reframe it as a project that is the equivalent of receiving $350,000 in grants from the National Institutes of Health that my client now doesn't have to apply for and win. Then I reframe that as being enough grant money to fund several more researchers' full-time salaries. In fact, since my gear will continue producing savings for twenty years, it's really the equivalent of giving that client seven million dollars in 'grants' that they don't have to apply for and win—all for the temporary inconvenience of working with me for a week or so to change out the lab's fume hood controls."

Granted, the seven million dollars back-of-the-envelope calculation considered neither inflation nor the time value of money. Still though, this reasoning was a really compelling way to connect the dots for a busy lab director who had to be convinced to invest the time and money to focus on something other than finding the cure for cancer (or whatever else his team happened to be working on at the time).

THE UNFORESEEN BENEFIT

Following up with your past customers allows you to not only confirm they received the benefits you promised them originally, but also discover if they experienced any unexpected benefits.

I was privileged to do a training session for a group of home performance contractors in New England. I asked the audience, "How many of you go back and talk to every customer to make sure that they received the benefits you promised them when you sold the job?" Less than half the audience raised their hands, which is not surprising. I then asked, "How many of you ask your customers if there were any benefits that they realized in the wake of the improvement that you had *not* promised them when selling the job?" Even fewer hands went up.

One of the few people who raised his hand said that he had asked this exact question to a woman who had hired him to do a whole-home insulation project. As expected, the insulation reduced her heating bill in the New England winter—but what she said next really caught this contractor's attention. She said, "You know, I was all about the energy savings, and seeing that come true was great. Everything worked out just as you said it would, but what's really interesting is that after you put that insulation in my wall, I could no longer hear the street noise—I can now watch my TV shows with the volume set three notches lower!"

Wouldn't it be awesome to have an *abundance of non-energy benefits* for each of your products or services that you could use to convince new prospects to buy? Make an effort to discover what unforeseen benefits your customers are appreciating in the wake of your completed projects and use that information to strengthen your value proposition for your next prospect.

"If it takes a lot of words to say what you have in mind,
give it more thought."
DENNIS ROTH

WHAT DO THEY REALLY WANT?

Let's face it: Energy efficiency is not always at the top of everyone's list of priorities. You may find yourself in a situation where your prospect doesn't think an efficiency upgrade is the best use of capital. What can you do in a case like this? Find out what *does* sit atop their list of priorities. You may not be able to help them fulfill their entire wish list. However, what if you reframed your efficiency offering and demonstrated that the value they would experience by approving your project would provide a path to achieving their most cherished goals?

I recently gave a keynote presentation on the East Coast for about five hundred energy controls specialists. Afterward, someone in the audience

approached me at the podium and shared a great story that exemplifies this kind of outside-of-the-box thinking.

He told me he had been trying to sell a school system on a major HVAC renovation project for many months. The district's budget director candidly shared, "Listen, improving our HVAC system is not our highest priority right now. What we're really focused on is our computerization initiative. We've already told our board that we're going to have 1,600 iPads by this time next year, one for each child in grades five and above. We think the iPad project will really help us see better learning outcomes in our district. Bottom line, we need to focus our attention on getting those iPads before we even think about any HVAC projects."

A typical salesperson would have heard that reasoning and said "Ugh, cross them off the list. This is never going to happen." A sales professional—which this person was—would not give up so easily. Sure enough, he said to the budget director, "Makes sense. Let me ask you though, do you have dollars already allocated to procure those iPads?" The director responded, "Well, we haven't figured that out yet, but we'll probably wind up leasing them from Apple."

This sales professional took it upon himself to go to Apple to see what such a lease would cost. Shortly thereafter, he came back to the district with a proposal. "I did a little research, and it turns out that you can lease those 1,600 iPads for 'x' dollars a month. And guess what? The monthly savings you'll enjoy once you install the HVAC improvements that I had originally proposed to you should more than cover the debt service on the iPads. Moreover, while your utility would never give you an incentive to reduce the first cost of those iPads, they *will* give you money to help you pay for those HVAC improvements, which will in turn generate enough savings to pay for those iPads! Bottom line, if you do what I'm suggesting, you'll be able to not only 'check the box' for the school board on the iPads, but also improve the thermal comfort of your classrooms, which—if I may speak frankly—will likely have a bigger positive impact on learning outcomes, student attendance, and perhaps even teacher attendance in your district than the bump you're hoping to see from those iPads."

Not surprisingly, this sales professional secured approval for his HVAC project shortly thereafter. Several weeks after he had closed the deal, he ran into a few of his competitors at a networking event. They couldn't believe the district had approved the HVAC project. "What? How did you pull that one off? We've been pitching them on an HVAC retrofit for nearly two years with virtually nothing to show for our efforts!" The sales professional dryly replied, "It wasn't an HVAC project; it was an iPad project," and then walked away, leaving his competitors scratching their heads.

This is exactly the kind of lateral thinking that you as an efficiency sales professional should be using with all of your prospects. As General Eisenhower once said, "Whenever I run into a problem I can't solve, I always try to make it bigger." He went on to explain that if he made the problem big enough, he could begin to see the outlines of a solution. In so many cases, the problem is not what you think it is. It is usually slightly beyond the margins of what you think you need to solve. Something else is interacting with the situation and causing it to be a problem. So *that* is what you should be doing—looking for the bigger or adjacent problem and solving it first.

"I would rather die of passion than of boredom."
VINCENT VAN GOGH

IS MY PRINTER LEAKING INK?

Ask anyone who sells efficiency solutions. We live in a world where one of the first questions a prospect asks when he or she hears about an energy-saving technology is "What's the payback?"

Now I ask you, if you're buying a piece of equipment that you're expecting to last "x" years, how much sense does it make to focus only on how the purchase price of that equipment compares to the savings you'll get in the first year? Think about it. What if one manufacturer's machine will last for five years while another manufacturer's machine will last for ten? What if one alternative is built less expensively, *with the expectation* that it will require higher maintenance over time?

I like to use the example of a laser printer versus an ink-jet printer because even the most unsophisticated prospects "get it." The laser printer will likely have a higher "first cost;" however, its cost per page of printing will likely be less. I have a friend who recently started a business and bought an inkjet printer, conscious of conserving his start-up capital. The business quickly grew, and he began churning through ink cartridges so fast that he said he was tempted to look under the machine and check for leaks!

On a similar note, if you buy an "inexpensive" laser printer, your savings in first cost will likely be offset with paper jams, higher maintenance costs, and probably a shorter lifetime as well.

Returning to our context of selling higher-cost, premium-efficiency equipment, the lesson we need to take away is that simple payback period is hardly the ticket to a wise decision.

"If everything's under control, you're going too slow."
MARIO ANDRETTI

IN THE ABSENCE OF MATH, DECISIONS ARE OFTEN GOVERNED BY MYTHS

Do not let fiction fill the vacuum left by a lack of facts. Blindly accepted myths and inappropriately applied "rules of thumb" play a major role in the continued waste of energy in this country. When selecting projects to fund, you need to know the facts. Who pays? Who benefits? You need access to tools that deliver actionable information automatically. If your financial analysis requires an impractical level of time and effort, it will not get done, especially if you need to see multiple scenarios before approving a project. If your people lack the time or skills to perform and present these calculations, you should consider outsourcing the financial analysis to someone who has automated the number-crunching.

In the case of a multi-tenant building, for example, are the people who approve capital projects the same people who approved the existing leases? If not, have they at least read the leases lately? How much of the energy cost is paid by the landlord? How much of the projected upgrade's savings would the landlord see on a tenant-by-tenant, month-by-month basis? Do the leases allow the landlord to assess tenants for capital improvements that reduce operating expenses for all tenants? If you are an engineer recommending an energy-saving capital project for a multi-tenant building, have you detailed the costs and savings of the project on a tenant-by-tenant and common-area basis? Do you know how much of the projected savings would flow to the landlord and how much capital cost could be assigned to the tenants according to the terms of the existing leases? Do you have a best practice of including a leasing analysis in every proposal you present to a landlord or manager of an income-producing property?

"It is in your moments of decision that
your destiny is shaped."
TONY ROBBINS

THE PERILS OF JUMPING
TO CONCLUSIONS

It's easy to jump to conclusions about why a reluctant buyer is not saying "yes." As a sales professional, it's your job to figure out exactly what prospects need to see or hear in order to eliminate their reservations.

Unfortunately, people are not always verbal on—or even aware of—the reasons for their reluctance. It's important not to jump to conclusions before you get to the bottom of it. The following efficiency sales story illustrates this concept:

The president of a large mechanical contractor (we'll call him Jonathan) attended one of our two-day Learning to S.E.E.: Sell Efficiency Effectively™ trainings. Midway through the seminar, he shared a story about a salesperson on his team who was trying to close a big sale. The prospect was not biting, so the salesperson dropped the price by nearly a half-million dollars. He was shocked to find that the prospect still wouldn't buy—even with the significantly lower price. (Hint: If you think price is the reason your prospect is not saying yes, you should read *Escaping the Price-Driven Sale* by Tom Snyder and Kevin Kearns. Its findings are the product of studying about a thousand sales situations to discover how often price was the deciding factor in winning the order. It's a real eye-opener.)

Anyway, Jonathan decided it was time to get involved. As the president of the firm, he set up a meeting with the prospect and through skillful questioning and observation, discovered the real reason the prospect hadn't said yes already. And guess what? It had nothing to do with price.

The salesperson was thrilled that his boss helped him close the deal. There was only one problem: Even though they had finally addressed what had been holding the prospect back and they were now ready to ink the deal, they were still stuck with the half-million-dollar discount that the salesperson had volunteered before he learned what the real problem was!

That salesperson—I intentionally say salesperson, not sales professional—didn't thoroughly evaluate the situation. If he had, he would have said to himself, "I'm *not* going to take a half-million dollars of my company's gross margin off the table just because I have a feeling that my prospect thinks the price is too high. I'm first going to see if there's anything *other than price* that might be preventing this prospect from giving us the green light on this project."

I heard the other day that the fastest-growing segment of the $200-million-dollar-a-year sales training industry is *business acumen training for salespeople*. This story certainly gives ample evidence of how an overzealous salesperson who doesn't understand the negative impact of surrendering a half-million dollars of gross margin could really damage his company's financial health, while being single-mindedly focused on boosting his own commissions.

Make sure your negotiating strategy doesn't just default to the lowest common denominator—"Let's just drop the price and see if that makes the prospect say yes." Rather, base your strategy on the answers you receive after carefully questioning what the prospect is really feeling. Jumping to conclusions without first thoughtfully assessing why your prospect hasn't already given you the green light will result in longer-than-necessary sales cycles and greatly reduced closing ratios.

"Live your life with a sense of positive expectancy."
MARK T. JEWELL

LESS IS MORE

Most sales professionals are asked to give presentations from time to time. If someone says you'll have sixty minutes to present, *do not* create sixty slides. What's going to happen if you have sixty slides? You'll be rushing through them, or worse yet, you'll be strolling through them very leisurely, perhaps getting derailed by a couple of offbeat questions and maybe even a personal story—and then you'll look up at the clock—and you'll be horrified to find that you have only twenty minutes remaining! You'll still have forty slides to get through, and it will be a disaster. Everybody in the audience will get increasingly uncomfortable. You won't have time to cover the remaining slides in sufficient detail, and your audience will grow increasingly anxious about

whether or not you'll be able to finish your presentation in time. Believe me, an anxious audience is lot less receptive to your ideas.

Now how do you make sure that you don't go over your allotted time (or have to rush through your slides)?

RULE #1: You practice your delivery.

RULE #2: If you're given an hour, you make about twenty-five minutes worth of slides.

Face it. You know you're going to start five or ten minutes late. You know you're going to be interrupted by a couple of questions. You know you're going to want to have Q&A at the end. You know you're going to want to have an open-ended discussion to take your audience's temperature after you finish your remarks. You should also factor in the possibility that one of your most valuable attendees may have to leave the meeting early. You really have to design your presentation with all of these contingencies in mind.

Here's a tip: Before you start delivering the presentation, check in to make sure you still have the agreed-upon time for the presentation. Also ask the audience directly if anyone expects to leave early. Probably 50 percent of the time, someone is going to pipe up and say, "Well, now that you mention it, I've got a plane to catch. I'll have to leave here about fifteen minutes early to catch my ride to the airport."

You should always "put the last slide first" because if that person is the ultimate decision-maker and you don't reach that point in your presentation before he has to leave early to catch that plane, believe me, you'll be kicking yourself the entire way home.

We could write an entire book on effective presentation techniques. In fact, the Efficiency Sales Professional™ Boot Camp features several modules on presenting effectively. For now though, let's just do a little math. Who came up with that rule of how many words to put on each slide: no more than five bullets, and no more than six words per bullet? This rule is absolutely ridiculous. Think about it. Five words times six bullets times sixty slides amounts to 1,800 words! That's more words than the average college term paper, and that's at a good school!

Do you really expect an audience to read the equivalent of an *entire college term paper*… over your shoulder… while you're talking… during the course of a single hour-long presentation… that starts late… and is interrupted by questions? Now we know why PowerPoint calls them "bullets." They kill audiences.

My favorite kind of presentation? All pictures. No words on the slides. Now *that* gets an audience's attention. Try it yourself. Be a storyteller, not a narrator. You'll be amazed. And so will your audience.

"It's not what you look at that matters, it's what you see."
HENRY DAVID THOREAU

ENERGY EFFICIENCY AND BUILDING VALUE

If you're selling efficiency solutions in the built environment, you may find yourself being asked by your prospects, "Will this energy efficiency upgrade increase the value of my building?" This can be a difficult question to answer because it varies from situation to situation. The first thing you should do is determine whether you're dealing with an owner-occupied building or a non-owner-occupied building.

In an owner-occupied building, there are at least two ways to connect enhanced energy efficiency to increased value. The first approach relates to the value of the real estate itself. If an appraiser notices that the building has been outfitted with state-of-the-art energy-efficient equipment, he will likely assign the building a higher value per square foot. Those improvements insulate the purchaser from deferred maintenance, technological obsolescence, future regulatory imperatives, occupant comfort issues, and similar concerns. The "cost approach" to appraisal should consider the quality of the installed systems. Moreover, the "market comparison approach" to appraisal should give the appraiser ample justification for adjusting the value per square foot higher when recently sold similar properties lacking those amenities are used for comparison.

The other way to connect the dots between enhanced efficiency and higher value focuses on *enterprise value* rather than the real estate itself. Let's assume you're a publicly traded company whose stock price is conditioned on earnings per share and the price-to-earnings ratio that the market has presently assigned to the company based on a variety of factors beyond the scope of this short essay. If energy efficiency lowers operating expenses, earnings increase—which means earnings per share increase—which means (at a stable P/E ratio) the share price increases— which means (at a constant number of shares outstanding) the market capitalization of the enterprise increases. Admittedly, a lot of dots to connect. However, the positive correlation between enhanced efficiency and higher enterprise value can be described, and this analysis doesn't even consider the earnings increase an enterprise may enjoy as a function of the non-utility-cost financial savings (e.g., productivity benefits resulting from improved thermal comfort, indoor air quality, etc.).

In income-producing buildings, connecting efficiency solutions to improved building value is a whole lot easier. The appraiser will likely focus on a number called "net operating income" (NOI). When the appraiser feels comfortable with that number, he is going to divide it by a market-considered capitalization rate. The higher the NOI, the higher the value of the building, assuming a stable cap rate. Perhaps you secured that higher net operating income by raising the rent (because the building is now more comfortable or the tenant's operating expenses are reduced). Perhaps the building enjoys higher occupancy (because the building is now more attractive to occupy, or more people renewed their leases). Perhaps you reduced the landlord's share of operating expenses. *As long as the NOI is higher,* the appraisal should reflect a higher value at a stable cap rate. That's what you need to do: increase NOI before the appraiser evaluates it. You needn't worry about whether the appraiser has the technical background to recognize a magnetic bearing chiller or variable frequency drives or whatever other efficiency enhancements that were installed.

Keep all of the above in mind and you'll be better prepared to demonstrate how your efficiency solution might very well support higher property value and/or enterprise value.

"Obstacles are those frightful things you see when you take your eyes off your goal."
HENRY FORD

WHAT SHOULD YOU FOCUS ON?

When you approach a prospect with a new project, you have a very limited amount of time to convince him or her that your product or service is a worthy investment of his or her time and money. For this reason, it's vital that you decide ahead of time *what* you're going to focus the conversation on. You can introduce your product or service in terms of its features, benefits, and/or value. Which of these should you focus on? Which of these is most likely to capture the attention of your prospect? Let's use an energy management system as an example:

What are some of the features? It can track up to "x" thousand control points; it handles minute modulations of temperature; and, it monitors and controls building loads.

What are the benefits? You can facilitate commissioning; you can provide visibility of equipment; you can gain insight into occupant comfort; and, you can enable automated demand response strategies in territories where it's worth doing.

What's the value? The public sees that you're a green company; you have a better handle on comfort and control; your occupants are happier, more productive, and more likely to stay; and, you get the ability to brag about an amenity that neighboring buildings don't have.

After reading the features, benefits, and value of this hypothetical energy management system, which category do you think a potential buyer would be most interested in discussing? I can confidently tell you that most people aren't going to buy the energy management system because of its features or even its benefits. Why? Features and benefits lack emotional appeal. Remember, most decisions are made emotionally and then justified financially. If you can connect the product or service with something that the prospect truly values and desires, you'll be miles ahead of the salesperson that squanders valuable selling time discussing technical specs and simple benefits.

"Perhaps imagination is only intelligence having fun."
GEORGE SCIALABBA

SELLING WITH STORIES AND REFERRALS

Telling a story about helping another customer is a great sales strategy. It demonstrates your willingness to be a Good Samaritan. It also feels great to be able to tell a prospect, "We do this all the time, and we can do it for you as well."

Having a list of referrals to provide is ideal. It reduces your prospects' perceived need to perform elaborate due diligence themselves. They take it for granted that the customers on that list already performed their own due diligence, and it's even more reassuring that they already used your product or service successfully.

Think about all the purchases you make—everything from cars to food to movie tickets. Think how comforting it is to hear someone else whose opinion you trust say, "I had a positive experience with that product."

Imagine for a moment what your life would be like without Consumer Reports, J.D. Powers, Yelp, or Amazon reviews. How much more difficult would your selections be if there were no five-star ratings? Without all of that proxy due diligence at your fingertips, could you even buy 10 percent of the stuff you now buy with confidence? Do yourself a favor. Assemble a large repertoire of positive stories and references to share with your prospects. It's a great way to help your prospects reach their own affirmative decisions with confidence.

"Striving for success without hard work is like trying to harvest where you haven't planted."

DAVID BLY

THE WINNING PRESENTATION

How do you prepare a presentation that will win over your audience? The first step is to contemplate the ways in which your audience might resist. I believe that repetition is the mother of learning, so if you anticipate the objections and you inoculate your presentation with the answers to those objections, you'll have a much more seamless approach to persuading somebody to do what you want them to do. Addressing these objections also demonstrates to your audience that you've carefully thought through everything, which will reduce their anxiety.

Ultimately, you need to determine the reward that would most resonate with each specific player in the decision-making process of an efficiency deal. If it's a sustainability director, it's the pride of removing thousands of tons of CO_2 emissions from the environment. If it's the chief financial officer, it might be providing greater certainty about budgeting and a hedge against utility price spikes. If it's the engineering department, it might be the reward of a phone that doesn't ring as frequently for hot/cold calls.

At the same time, you might have some purpose-driven CEOs, like the chap who runs Whole Foods, willing to entertain a conversation about how putting refrigerator door seals and LED lights in and doing all sorts of other wonderful things for his supermarkets will have a positive impact on the environment. The person who runs Patagonia—similar conversation.

Just realize that there are some people who do things just for themselves, some who do things for their organization selflessly, and others who ultimately do selfless things for mankind. It's your job to figure out what you're up against and to prepare a presentation that will preemptively address your audience's objections and cater to their desires.

"Successful people do what unsuccessful people
are not willing to do."
JEFF OLSON

THE RELUCTANT BUYER

Too many salespeople give their prospects reasons to talk themselves out of a purchase. Your job as a sales professional is to make sure they don't find a reason *not* to buy.

Let's say you have a prospect interested in purchasing window film for his building. Chances are he's never touched window film in his life—except perhaps unintentionally while pressing his nose against the glass of a store window to see what they sell. He has no idea what window film looks like, tastes like, smells like, or feels like—nor what it costs to install. He certainly has no clue as to how many grades of window film are available for purchase.

The prospect simply says, "I think I need some window film." The average salesperson could reply, "Well, you've come to the right place. We have virtually every grade of window film under the sun (pun intended). Here are the seventeen grades of window films for which I can show you samples right here. We have another twenty options in our warehouse. Take a look at these. Which one do you like best?"

In an effort to offer ultimate variety so the prospect would find no need to shop elsewhere, the salesperson has unintentionally paralyzed the decision-maker. The prospect is now thinking, "Seventeen choices? That means there are at least sixteen chances I could make the wrong decision. And that's not even considering the other twenty choices in this guy's warehouse, wherever that is. Holy cow, how am I going to pick the right one? I really should find a window film consultant, but I don't even know where to find one of those, much less how much they'd charge me to evaluate all of my options. I guess I'll just ask some of my neighbors at the next Building Owners and Managers Association meeting who they wound up using for window films and what variety they finally installed."

Meanwhile, the purchase is in suspended animation. Who would feel confident buying a whole building's worth of window film where the odds of choosing the right product are only one in seventeen?

A sales professional would have said, "I would be happy to help you choose the right solution. First, let me ask you, where were you thinking of installing this film, and what is your main reason for doing so? Privacy? Avoiding heat gain? Protecting your merchandise from fading?"

Equipped with the answers to those questions, the sales professional would then recommend two or three window films that best fit the need, making it easier for the prospect to be confident he was making the right decision.

REFERRAL FOLLOW-UP

When someone gives you a referral, it's important that you follow up immediately—not only to thank them, but also to find out *why* they gave you a referral. You might think that it sounds self-deprecating or overly modest to ask, "Why?" Actually, it's not. You want to know which aspects of your sales delivery mechanism impressed that person enough to refer you.

Your client may say, "Oh, you were Johnny on the spot. You handled my request quickly, and I actually have a friend who could really benefit from your service right away. You've got to call him today." Or, they may say, "What I really liked about your approach was that you were really patient with me. Even though it took us six months to decide, you were there with us every step of the way." Or, "You were the only company that had both this and that."

So now you know going into it how you've been praised by the individual who referred you, and you can highlight those attributes when you actually get in touch with the person to whom you were referred. It tells you what they most value about your business at that point in time. It is invaluable information to have in hand *before* calling the referral, so don't be afraid to ask (right after you say, "Thank you!").

"The key is not to prioritize what's on your schedule, but to schedule your priorities."
STEPHEN COVEY

THE PROJECTOR AS
MODERN-DAY CAMPFIRE

What is the structure of an effective presentation? Well, not surprisingly, it has a beginning, a middle, and an end. The beginning is the call to adventure. The middle, of course, is the contrast—*what is* versus *what could be*. The end is a call to action. The three sections have to have a clear focus or the audience will tune you out. A focused presentation has a primary intention and no more than three or four main ideas to surround that primary intention. If you keep the presentation focused, people will know where you're going and follow you there.

You also have to keep it interesting. How do you do that? Photographs are interesting. Contrast is interesting. People are interesting. Stories are interesting. Case studies are interesting. What is not interesting? Cut sheets. Technical specifications. Units of measure that most people don't know the meaning of: kilowatts, kilowatt-hours, therms, and so forth.

If you throw in some drama, that helps, too. Don't be afraid to make it personal. In her book, *Resonate: Present Visual Stories that Transform Audiences* (which I highly recommend), Nancy Duarte talks about how the PowerPoint presentation is the modern version of a campfire. She notes that, unfortunately, most people who use this "4,500-lumen campfire" are simply not adept storytellers.

Would you like to keep your audience huddled around your campfire rapt with attention? Then keep your presentation concise, structured, and visually engaging. Focus on attention-grabbing contrast. Tell a few stories with memorable punch lines. Do all that and you'll have the audience in the palm of your hand, rather than just your slide advancer!

"The right word may be effective, but no word was ever as effective as a rightly timed pause."

MARK TWAIN

UNLOCK IT

Sales professionals often ask me what format is best to use when sending a proposal digitally. While it may seem like a good idea to send a locked document (as a way of protecting intellectual property), I think it's almost always better to send proposals as an unlocked PDF.

Why PDF? Because you can't guarantee that your recipient's machine has all of the fonts you used. The PDF will portray your document the way it appeared on your own computer screen, rather than having one of your fancy fonts replaced by a generic font like Courier, which would make your document look more like a ransom letter from the Seventies than a proposal! Moreover, have you ever made the mistake of sending a Word document to your prospect, only to discover that someone in your office forgot to "Accept All Changes" after using the proposal you sent to your prospect's competitor as the template for this proposal? Yikes.

And why "unlocked"? Ideally, the person to whom you send the proposal will circulate it broadly to other decision-makers in the chain. You took the time to create perfectly worded prose. Making it easy for your prospect to copy and paste that prose directly into a management memo or capital budgeting request reduces the amount of work you're expecting your prospect to do, while increasing the probability that the proposal will be approved. Besides, let your prospect take the credit for having written it. They might earn a pat on the head or even a performance bonus at the end of the year.

In most cases, the person to whom you send your proposal is not really getting approval for *you*; they're getting approval to do the project. Ultimately, it doesn't matter whether the persuasive language from your proposal is attributed to you or to the person passing your message along internally as long as it does the trick, right? Once your internal champion gets approval, he'll come back to you and say, "Great! *We* got the project approved."

"The state of your life is nothing more than a reflection of the state of your mind."
WAYNE DYER

ASK FOR THE REFERRAL

We all know how valuable referrals are for generating new business. One of the best times to ask for a referral is right after the sale (or once the installation is complete). They bought your product or service, they're happy with their decision, and you haven't done anything wrong yet.

They're more likely to give you a referral if you frame it as a win-win situation: "John, I have a question for you. Can you think of anyone else in your circle of friends and colleagues who could benefit from...?" As you complete the sentence, pay close attention to the wording. You might complete the question with, "...having the same sort of enhanced visibility into energy usage that you now have throughout your portfolio?" Focus on the value that caused your customer to buy. Not features. Not benefits. *Value.* You want to know if anyone else your customer knows might appreciate the same value. This is no time for haphazard word choice. You don't want to come across as saying some variant of, "Do you know anyone else who might want to buy some controls from me so that I could earn another commission?"

Asking the question in the manner originally suggested plants the idea in the customer's mind that they could be of genuine service to a friend by offering them something they know is worth the investment. They get to prove to other people that they were smart enough to find you and implement your solution. You give them social currency by allowing them to be a hero in the eyes of the person they choose to refer. As much as receiving a referral may benefit you financially, don't make it about you—make it about *them.*

"We don't get a chance to do that many things, and every one should be really excellent. Because this is our life."

STEVE JOBS

TIPS FOR PITCHING

Every efficiency sales professional should have a handful of "elevator pitches" prepared, each one customized for a specific audience type. Here are some things to keep in mind as you prepare your elevator pitches:

Your elevator pitch should be:
- Short and to the point
- Humorous
- Memorable
- Interactive (say something and pause for a response or ask a question)
- Conversational

Your elevator pitch should not be:

- A scripted speech
- A pitch (in the traditional "sales pitch" sense)
- Longer than fifteen seconds

Avoid fluff words that don't really mean anything:

- "Finest"
- "Established"
- "Foremost"
- "Leading"
- "Pioneering"
- "Original"

*"What you do makes a difference, and you have to decide
what kind of difference you want to make."*

JANE GOODALL

WHY STOP WITH A SINGLE PRESS?

Have you maximized the revenue potential of your customer base? Do you have customers who could really benefit from some of your newer products or services? Take a few minutes right now to think about how you might close new sales with existing customers.

For the sake of analogy, imagine that your customers are olives. You want to make sure that for every olive that you touch, you don't just press it once to get the extra virgin olive oil. You press it again to get the next grade of oil, and then again to get the next grade after that. Only after it's been reduced to a dry pulp do you toss that olive in the compost pile or perhaps feed it to the farm animals. The moral of the story? Too many salespeople in the efficiency business just go for the first press and then move on. That's a tremendous squandering of potential revenue, right?

How do you make sure that *you're* not doing what I just described? Well, you measure account performance quantitatively: perhaps the number of transactions or total revenues generated per customer over the last fiscal year.

Let's make it personal: What were *your* average number of transactions and revenues per customer last year?

If you work at a company with multiple salespeople, here's a great agenda item for your next sales meeting: Challenge each of your colleagues to research and calculate the highest number of transactions and the highest amount of revenues he or she attained with a single customer in the last twelve months. In a group of ten salespeople, you'll likely see a range: "One sale." "Seven sales." "Three sales." The spread on revenues per customer will likely be even more pronounced.

Once you hear the figures, you'll find yourself asking, "Wait a second. What did you do to get seven sales out of the same customer in a single fiscal year?"

"Well, I did this and this… and oh, I did that as well."

What's the next sentence out of your mouth? If you're the sales manager, it had better be: "Mr. One Sale, your job is to take Mr. Seven Sales to lunch this week so he can explain to you what he does to nurture relationships through account development. And how about this: I'll pick up the tab for your lunch, and you can pick up the tab for all of the incremental income tax you're going to be paying this coming year once you start applying what Mr. Seven Sales is going to tell you he's already doing to turbocharge his own commissions!"

F.E.A.R.:
FUNNY EMOTION AROUND RISK

Fear can prevent us from pursuing what we really want in life. It can prevent us from starting our own businesses, making those cold calls to hot prospects, or asking for referrals, even though we know in our hearts that we really deserve them.

The good news is that there are plenty of examples in our culture where overcoming the fear of failure has yielded great rewards. We hear stories all the time about how the most successful people have experienced the most failure—how Steve Jobs made huge mistakes and failed—how the greatest inventors of all time had the largest or most frequent flops. When

is the last time you heard about a truly great dream materializing without someone taking a few well-calculated risks along the way?

Here are a few tips for conquering the fears that may be standing between *you* and high performance:

- **Have a plan**—You'll be more confident and more likely to succeed if you have a carefully conceived plan. If you're thinking about making the leap to running your own business, make sure you have a solid business plan that's been well vetted by people who aren't afraid to give you "tough love" feedback on its merits. Before you pick up the phone to call the big fish, make sure you've run through what you'll say and that you've planned your responses to questions or objections they may have. Before you ask for a referral, take the time to plan the best opportunity for doing so. A previous installment of the "Jewell Insights" blog listed no less than six situations that are ideal times to ask for a referral. Feel free to check out the "Jewell Insights" blog archive online if you're scratching your head right now wondering what those six situations might be!

- **Visualize Success**—Taking the time to visualize a successful outcome is imperative. In fact, if you can't visualize success, you need to take a step back and ask yourself why. The first person you need to convince is yourself. We teach our efficiency sales professionals to visualize all five senses of the successful outcome: what it will look like, feel like, sound like, taste like, and even smell like. A richly visualized outcome can fool your brain into thinking that the positive outcome has already happened. Did you ever close your eyes and visualize biting into a lemon, only to find your mouth salivating as if you had already done so? As powerful as it is, the human brain often has difficulty distinguishing between what is real and what is imagined—and that's a good thing when you're visualizing successful outcomes.

- **Remember that your action will not determine the rest of your life.** Woody Allen used to have such performance anxiety that before he'd walk out on stage to do his stand-up act, he'd close his eyes and repeat to himself, "Nothing I do tonight will influence my career in any way." A mentor of mine once told me that if you just do the right thing all the time, sooner or later you'll do it at the right time, at which point you'll finally enjoy the success you deserve. Another mentor once highlighted the difference between distress and eustress (a termed coined by endocrinologist Hans Selye to describe "good stress"). Too much stress can lead to a suboptimal outcome; however, a little anxiety can actually empower higher performance.

I keep a small metal plaque on my desk that says, "What would you attempt to do if you knew you could not fail?" Can you imagine how much happier and more impactful *you* would be if you adopted this attitude in your own life? Just do it. You'll wonder why you didn't start living by this motto years ago.

"Wisdom is the reward you get for a lifetime of listening when you'd have preferred to talk."
DOUG LARSON

GOING THE EXTRA MILE

Selling efficiency takes perseverance, creativity, and a willingness to go the extra mile. Here's a story about a colleague (we'll call him Nick) who did just that to close an important sale.

Nick was proposing to retrofit a small city's street lighting with LED heads. The project made a lot of sense both economically and environmentally. Unfortunately, he faced resistance from the city's public works director who told him, "Sounds great in theory, but we can't do it because we don't know how many street lights we actually have. The Streets Department knows its records are off, and although the utility invoices us each month for the number of pole connections it says we have, we're pretty sure it doesn't have the right inventory either. Bottom line: We don't want to take on a project when we don't really know how many LED replacement heads we need to buy."

Now you're probably thinking, "For goodness sake, how far apart could the city and utility's estimates of street lights be? Besides, why not just ask vendors to quote the job with add/deduct unit pricing and make sure the contract specifies the maximum number of fixtures that are authorized for retrofit?"

After advancing these or similar arguments in vain, most salespeople would probably walk away, defeated before they began. Nick, however, was a true sales professional. He was not about to leave this project undone. So what did he do? That weekend, he jumped in his pickup truck with a friend who agreed that the task that they were about to undertake was both crazy and cool. The two of them literally drove each and every street within the city limits and counted every single street light! That's right. Every darned one of them.

With his newly minted street light inventory in hand, Nick knew he could create a compelling proposal. The city could now rest assured that it had an accurate count. Perhaps even more importantly, the public works director owed Nick and his buddy a debt of gratitude for producing in a single weekend something that neither the Streets Department nor the utility had been able to deliver for years.

Sometimes you have to play the adult in a relationship and go the extra mile to make people play nice. Sometimes you need to do some lateral thinking and serve as the catalyst, because left to their own devices, too many prospects would remain in their respective silos and never get their act together. It's not always easy. However, if you collect the right data at the right time and present it in a persuasive way, you might just turn a skeptical prospect into a true believer.

THE CORRECT RESPONSE TO THE WRONG REQUEST

Too many salespeople tell every prospect the same thing, either because they're lazy or because they're not taking the time to evaluate each prospect's particular situation and needs. As a result, those salespeople fail to deliver messages that truly resonate with their prospects. The result? An unnecessarily low closing ratio.

I remember reading a fabulous story about this concept of telling people what they really need to hear. The story described a sales professional who was offering a complicated service in the context of a complex bid process where the final step was making a one-hour formal presentation to the folks who would ultimately select the winning bidder. His competing bidders had squandered their respective one-hour presentations, essentially reading a synopsis of their proposals.

This final bidder, however, took quite a different tack. In the opening minute of the meeting he said, "Everybody else probably came here and read you their proposal. We have more respect for you than that. We know that you can read. What I'd like to do is spend the next fifty-nine minutes telling you what *should* have been in your request for proposal (RFP), and how much exposure you'll have if you select a bidder based on the requirements and evaluation criteria as they now stand in your RFP."

What do you think happened? Everyone in the room listened very intently. They soon realized how many blind spots they had failed to anticipate when drafting their RFP. Not surprisingly, they canceled the original RFP, and the one that took its place was very much in line with the changes recommended by this final bidder. Once the new RFP was out on the street, it was an obvious choice to select the bidder who had opened the prospect's eyes to the shortcomings of the original one.

This is yet another example of the effectiveness of being a challenger, rather than a relationship-builder. Look for ways to customize your offering to better fit the needs of your prospects, and don't be afraid to challenge their expectations. They'll likely thank you for it in the end.

"The best vision is insight."
MALCOLM FORBES

DON'T FEAR THE C-SUITE

A lot of people are uncomfortable selling to the C-Suite (Chief Financial Officer, Chief Operating Officer, Chief Executive Officer, etc.). Why? I think one of the main reasons people are intimidated is that they haven't had much experience interacting with that level of executive, and therefore they have little or no insight into what those folks get paid to do.

Just remember, C-level folks are human beings. And it doesn't take too much mental gymnastics to imagine what they care about. For example, if you find yourself addressing a CEO, here are two of the most important questions you should be answering in your presentation: "How will my offering make this organization easier to manage?" and "How will my offering make this enterprise more valuable?" Think about it. The Board of Directors hired the CEO to answer those two questions on a daily basis. Your job is to help that CEO connect the dots between your offering and a better answer to those two questions. His job depends on it. And so does your sale.

With all that in mind, be sure to keep your presentation concise.

And remember, the higher up you get on the corporate ladder, the less price matters. Demonstrate how your offering can make your prospect's organization easier to manage and more valuable. Price can come later—and only after you have convinced your prospect of your offering's true value.

"You've got to think about big things while you're doing small things so that all the small things go in the right direction."

ALVIN TOFFLER

IT'S TIME TO GET VISUAL

With the ever-present stimulation and fast pace of modern society comes the decline of attention span. If you want to capture the attention of a prospect who doesn't have the attention span (or ability) to fully understand a formal written proposal with its complex financial and technical appendices, consider adding some visuals to convey value.

I heard a story several years ago about a campaign created by J. C. Penney to transform the behavior of its tens of thousands of store associates:

J. C. Penney hypothesized that behavioral modification was a great way to save energy, so they spent $50,000 to hire a professional cartoonist to create a comic book that featured caricatures of the energy manager and all of the C-level executives at the company. They even created fictional characters like "Energy Man" to guide readers through the story of how their associates could actually have a meaningful impact on the energy management of a typical store with zero capital investment. Prizes were given to the stores that saved the most energy—simple stuff, like pizza parties, "Extreme Energy Makeovers" of staff break rooms with ENERGY STAR®-labeled appliances, and tiny cash bonuses for the managers of high-scoring stores. They called the campaign "March Utility Madness" to coincide with college basketball season.

The first time they circulated the comic book, they saved $500,000 in corporate energy *in one month*. That was a ten-to-one return. Wondering whether it was a fluke, they did a similar campaign the next year and saved *another* half a million dollars.

These savings were the result of people proactively applying common sense to energy-related aspects of their stores' operation. They turned the escalators off as soon as the store closed; switched the jewelry case lighting off at the end of the day because no one was going to be selecting jewelry to purchase when the store is closed; turned parking lot lighting off during daytime hours; etc. With simple steps like these and a friendly sense of comedic competition, J. C. Penney was able to save a tremendous amount of energy and money. The last I heard, the chain had saved more than $4 million in energy repeating this simple campaign year after year.

Words are not always the most effective vehicle for creating a compelling need for change. Sometimes it pays to get visual.

PREVAILING AT A PREMIUM

'd like to share a story that I remember reading a few years ago in a trade magazine about a "rock star" roofing contractor and his particular approach for convincing a price-sensitive prospect to buy a higher first-cost, premium-quality installation.

As I recall, the interviewer asked the contractor, "What do you say to a prospect when he tells you he's received a lower bid from another roofer?" His response was something along the lines of, "I tell my customers that when you're in the roofing business, Johns Manville and all the other manufacturers sell raw materials to everybody in the industry at basically the same price. So if someone's quoting you a higher price for an installation, it's likely they're planning to apply more supervisory hours, use more highly skilled labor, carry more than sufficient levels of liability insurance, etc. If you have a roofer that says he's willing to do the job for $3,000 versus my bid of $3,800, you have to ask yourself a question: What do you think the $800 is paying for that *you're not going to get* with the $3,000 roofing job? And while we're on the topic, if your 'bargain roofer' has trimmed his price at the expense of having workers' comp insurance, and one of his uninsured workers slips and falls off your roof, that worker would likely sue you—you could lose your home."

He concluded, "By the time I get done explaining even a few of the many ways 'cheaper' contractors cut corners to deliver their lower prices, the prospect is so nervous, they realize that even if they *could* save $800 on the job, they'd likely stay awake at night for the next ten years wondering what shortcuts that cheaper roofer took." And do you know what? His closing ratio was exceptionally higher than normal, despite the fact (or perhaps *because* of the fact) that his prices were routinely higher than his competition's.

It's all about how you frame your price and convey the genuine value of your service—even if it's just superior peace of mind knowing that the job will be done well. You've heard me say it before: Customers don't make decisions, they make comparisons. It's up to you to frame the comparison so that selecting you as the winning bidder is the only decision they could make and not regret later.

There's a second moral to this story, by the way. I encourage you to look for success stories and tips from sales rock stars in other industries, particularly those adjacent to the efficiency industry, to find new ideas to grow your own revenues.

COAX AND JOKE

In order to turn a skeptical prospect into a buyer, it often takes more than just a compelling proposal and persuasive financials. A sales professional needs to know how to push a prospect—without being "pushy." So how do you give that much-needed nudge without sending your prospect over the cliff? Try a little humor.

Laughter is one of the ways your body releases stress. I heard it explained many years ago that if the human mind encounters two planes of reasoning that inexplicably collide, the tension that results is often reconciled through laughter. The example given was a vaudeville act where a man dressed as a highly decorated general authoritatively struts out on stage—and proceeds to slip on a banana peel! The audience bursts into laughter because the notion of a person of such authority succumbing to such an obstacle trips a circuit breaker in the mind.

I analogize coaxing a prospect to do something that they would not normally do to "bending a branch." Every time you sense you are nearing the breaking point, you release the pressure. Repeating this regimen of applying pressure, releasing the pressure, and then applying pressure again allows you to bend a branch much farther than if you had simply applied ever-increasing pressure—an approach that would probably result in the branch breaking. Alternatively, in the absence of any bending force, you would be looking at a straight stick!

Applying pressure and then releasing it with humor can be extremely effective when asking your prospect to leave her comfort zone (e.g., suggesting that she fund expense reducing capital projects with longer paybacks). Ask the prospect to bend too far too fast and the conversation will end unproductively. If you fail to ask the prospect to bend at all, you will lose the sale. You need the right mix of pressure and release to move a reluctant prospect toward a fruitful outcome.

If you use this approach effectively, you will greatly increase the probability of convincing your prospect to do something he or she never would have considered previously. As long as your efficiency solution is genuinely beneficial, that would be a win-win, and your prospect will likely thank you for it after becoming your customer.

"The most difficult thing is the decision to act.
The rest is merely tenacity."
AMELIA EARHART

REGISTRY OF BUILDINGS

One of the resources that we always recommend for finding prospects and conveying the true value of your efficiency products and services is the ENERGY STAR® registry of certified buildings and plants. This resource lists all ENERGY STAR®-certified buildings and is searchable by location, building type, and year of certification.

Why is this valuable? For one, you can figure out which buildings have already recognized the value of measuring what they're managing. These are potential targets because you can be certain that these building owners and managers understand the value of efficiency improvements. You can also use the process of deduction to figure out which buildings have *not* made efficiency improvements. Using a similar ENERGY

STAR®-labeled building as an example, you can target a specific inefficient building and cite the labeled building as a success story to emulate.

I heard a fabulous story from one of our Efficiency Sales Professional™ Boot Camp graduates. He said that when he was given the responsibility of rolling out new utility efficiency programs, he'd first research the service territory's top-rated buildings (e.g., those with LEED® credentials) and request a tour of the physical plant. Why? Because while a layman might think that a LEED Gold building has no improvement potential remaining, the reality is often surprising. This particular sales professsional said that as he was given a tour of the building by the chief engineer, his host almost invariably mentioned how some shortcut had been taken on the road to attaining LEED certification, how he'd really like to improve this or that system now that he's seen it in action, etc. Many of those side comments became the thin edge of the wedge for suggesting additional efficiency improvements.

Keep in mind that the energy intensity seen in an ENERGY STAR® building that squeaked by with a score of 75 is typically much higher than what you'd see in a building with a score of 99. Don't assume that buildings sporting ENERGY STAR® labels have no remaining potential for improvement. In fact, they may represent some of the best buildings in the community to approach because their owners and managers appreciate the value of benchmarking *and* they already have a system in place to prove on a normalized basis the positive impact of any subsequent upgrades.

I highly recommend browsing through this EPA database and brainstorming some creative ways to utilize the information.

WHY DO THEY SAY "YES"?

Why might your prospect be willing to say "yes" to taking on a proposed energy-efficiency project? Is it about saving energy? Saving money? Saving carbon? Something else?

No doubt there are dozens of reasons a prospect might be motivated to say "yes" to pursuing your energy-saving project. I encountered one of the more surprising ones the other day when a workshop participant told me that her municipal client agreed to do a project because if they didn't find something for one of their managers to work on, they'd have to lay him off. It wasn't about saving the energy itself, the economic value, or the carbon content. It was all about saving their valued team member from the ravages of unemployment.

Seth Godin is a world-renowned author of more than a dozen books on marketing, consumer behavior, and similar topics. He once wrote a blog called "A hierarchy of business-to-business needs" that gives excellent insight into what motivates a "yes."

Seth wrote that if you're selling a product or service to a non-business owner in a business-to-business setting, the primary needs rank as follows:

* Avoiding risk
* Avoiding hassle
* Gaining praise
* Gaining power
* Having fun
* Making a profit

How does the typical energy-efficiency proposal fare when juxtaposed to that hierarchy? Well, let's think about it.

How much *risk* does a manager take on by saying "yes" to a fifty-plus page proposal written in another industry's technical jargon?

How much *hassle* is involved in understanding all of the competing technologies and approaches, interviewing and then selecting suppliers, negotiating contracts, applying for and securing the necessary capital, filling out incentive applications, cooperating with pre- and post-installation walk-throughs, measuring actual savings against projections, etc.—all for the purpose of replacing equipment that is not technically "broken"?

And skipping down to the bottom of Seth's hierarchy, how might the resulting energy efficiency map into the last item: *making a profit*? How similar is "saving energy" to "making a profit"? And how much is the estimated savings? Would it even "move the needle" when compared with the rest of the organization's overhead? Who would actually receive the savings? And would that be the same person who had to endure all of the above-referenced risk and hassle?

I recently read that more than 70 percent of American workers were "disengaged." Another recently published study warned that on any given day, half the workforce is looking for another job, either casually or formally. Can you imagine their perspective on taking on additional risk or hassle when, even if the project were successful, their "reward" would be their employer making more profit?

I mentioned all of this in a recent Efficiency Sales Professional™ Boot Camp, and someone wryly pointed out that the middle-ranked motivators—gaining praise, gaining power—still applied even if you were seeking other employment. Why? A successful energy project is a great resume builder! Reducing your present employer's energy bills or capturing an ENERGY STAR® label for the facility you now manage could be a feather in your cap while interviewing for a new role.

One thing is for sure, whether your prospect is looking for another job or not: Someone who has the insight to connect the dots between enhanced energy efficiency and more traditional metrics of performance (think better productivity in office environments, lower scrap rate in industrial settings, better learning outcomes in schools, etc.) stands to receive praise and maybe even more power and influence within their organization by aggressively pursuing an efficiency agenda.

So what are the morals to this story? I see at least three:

- Never assume the reason that your prospect is interested in your offerings is as simple as saving energy or even money.
- Realize that decision-makers are human beings first and job titles second.
- Leverage the above-referenced Seth Godin hierarchy as you formulate compelling value propositions for your prospects. How? Well, how about these for starters:
    - ◇ Reduce the risk: Bring industry foreknowledge to the table— genuine insight into how your solution has provided value for others in your prospect's situation and how your offerings compare to the competition's. Doing so will reduce the perceived risk of whatever you are proposing and help the prospect feel more comfortable proceeding without undertaking extensive due diligence.
    - ◇ Minimize the hassle: Make it easy to do business with you to reduce the perceived hassle factor. Act as a broker of strengths and coordinate your efforts with other vendors, if necessary.
    - ◇ Offer promise of praise: Offer to write a success story—or perhaps help the prospect apply for the ENERGY STAR® label— after the proposed project is successfully implemented.
    - ◇ Draw a path to increased power: Help the prospect see how moving forward positions him or her more favorably in the organization. The above-referenced success story might also help the prospect justify a raise or promotion!
    - ◇ Have fun: Wow, this point has so many dimensions, it deserves its own installment of the Jewell Insights blog! Here's just one to think about in the meantime: Make the effort to discover what the prospect finds truly fun and fascinating about his or her job, and then make sure your selling approach resonates with those preferences. Let's say your prospect enjoys escaping the office

for the occasional "field trip." You might suggest a lunch at their favorite eatery, bookended by two tours of buildings already benefiting from your offering. Above all, be eternally positive and personable, have a great sense of humor, and use it often. By the way, if you don't have a sense of humor, get one! Your prospects want to be around people who make them feel great!

◇ Demonstrate the true value: Take the time to connect the dots between efficiency and segment-specific outcomes that are more valuable than the cost of the kilowatts, kilowatt-hours, or therms saved. Remember, there are three distinct categories of benefits to highlight when selling efficiency solutions: utility-cost financial benefits (utility bill savings plus any rebates or other financial incentives); non-utility-cost financial benefits (e.g., the value of increased productivity when your solution delivers improved occupant comfort and convenience in addition to the energy savings); and, non-financial benefits (e.g., earning an ENERGY STAR® label). Keep in mind that in some cases, the third category blurs into the second one—for example, when an ENERGY STAR®-labeled building commands higher rent per square foot, a higher occupancy rate, or a higher sales price per square foot when compared to its non-labeled peers.

There's certainly a lot to be learned about advancing efficiency from one of the world's most respected marketing geniuses.

"Sometimes the best helping hand you can get is a good, firm push."
JOANN THOMAS

PAINT A NEW PICTURE

One of the most common roadblocks to a successful sale is a prospect or customer with *unrealistic expectations*. People have a tendency to expect things to be the same as they've always been.

This idea reminds me of the story of a little girl who goes to a multi-generational family dinner. The mother is cooking a huge ham. She cuts the end of the ham off, lays it in the pan, and puts it in the oven. The little girl says, "Mommy, why do you always cut off the end of the ham before you lay it in the pan and put it in the oven?" The mother tells her, "I don't know. That's what my mommy always did. Look there, grandma's out in the parlor talking to your sister. Why don't you go out and ask her?"

She goes out and asks, "Grandma, why does mommy always cut off the end of the ham before she lays it in the pan and puts it in the oven?" Grandma says, "I don't know, honey. That's the way my mommy always taught me to do it. She's outside with the dog. Why don't you ask her?"

So the little girl trundles out to the yard and says, "Great-grandma, why does everybody in this family cut off the end of the ham before they lay it in the pan and put it in the oven?" Great-grandma says, shaking her head, "I don't know, child. I did it because the ham didn't fit in my pan."

People often make decisions based on what they're accustomed to, without grounding those decisions in reality. When it comes to justifying an efficiency project financially, this can be a problem for us as sales professionals. You may have prospects tell you that they'll only do a project with a payback of two years or less, for example. Why do they have such unrealistic expectations? Probably because they were doing business in the Eighties, when the prime rate hit 21 percent. It's your job to paint a new picture for them—to be the "great-grandma" who reveals the reason for their unrealistic expectations and explains why they shouldn't dismiss your proposal, given how genuinely attractive it is as compared to other investment vehicles in today's market.

"We are what we repeatedly do. Excellence, therefore, is not an act but a habit."

ARISTOTLE

SELLING VALUES, NOT FEATURES OR BENEFITS

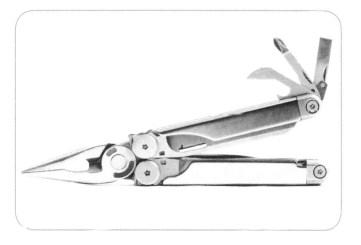

There's an age-old saw (pun intended) about selling benefits rather than features. Guess what? You shouldn't be selling benefits either! You should be selling the *value*.

I like to use the Leatherman® tool as an example: Why do people buy a Leatherman? Do they buy it because it has scissors, tweezers, a toothpick, a corkscrew, and a saw, all in the same tool? Do they really fall in love with the Phillips head screwdriver or the can opener? No. These are just *features* of the product.

Do they buy it because it can open a bottle of wine, cut some wire, or saw a large branch? No. These are just *benefits* of owning a Leatherman.

People buy a Leatherman because it is congruent with their *values*. Maybe they value the sense of having everything they need, right in their back pocket, whenever they need it. Maybe they buy it because it makes them feel like MacGyver. Maybe they want the opportunity to fix something on the spot and look like a hero in front of their date. Maybe they don't have room for a whole box of hand tools in their tiny apartment. Values cause prospects to become buyers. Not features. Not benefits. *Values.*

So how does this relate to selling efficiency? Take a high-tech lighting control system, for example. Does your prospect buy features—a certain number of control points and dimming ballasts? How about benefits—the ability to dim to a certain brightness or shed 25 percent of the lighting load during a demand-response emergency? Or is the prospect motivated by gaining greater control in general? Control boosts employee morale and productivity by allowing them to set their own lighting levels. Control allows the building owner to feel that he or she now has some options if an unforeseen demand-response event were to triple the cost per kilowatt-hour.

Ultimately, you have to ask yourself two questions: "What is my prospect really buying?" and, "What should I really be selling?"

Once you discover the *value* your prospect perceives, you shouldn't be selling anything else. If they're buying lower lighting power density, then guess what? That's what you should be talking about. However, I bet that's not what's motivating the purchase, which means you need to be talking about something entirely different.

WATCH YOURSELF

From the minute you step through the door to meet with a prospect, you're being evaluated on your appearance and demeanor. No matter how valuable your product or service is, if your prospect detects something amiss, your odds of closing the sale plummet. So how do you make sure you're making the best possible impression? *Videotape yourself.*

Professionals whose livelihoods depend on credible performances (television reporters, for example) know that practicing in front of a video camera is the best way to recognize and eliminate any unconscious behaviors that might be off-putting to their viewers.

Sales professionals should do the same. I recommend videotaping and evaluating yourself from two different perspectives:

- ◆ Watch yourself with the audio muted. You might notice distracting ticks, strange (or even blank) facial expressions, and other nervous habits.
- ◆ Listen to the audio without watching the video. Perhaps you had an energetic and dynamic physical presence, but your speech is monotonic. Perhaps your choice of words is not ideal. Perhaps you speak too quickly, forget to breathe, use the words "like" or "um," etc.

Experiencing the audio and video tracks separately will give you the insight you need to hone your craft and become a more powerful presenter.

"Turn your face to the sun and the shadows fall behind you."
MAORI PROVERB

TIPS FOR TALKING TO A PROSPECT

Over the course of my career as a sales professional, I've steadfastly adhered to certain best practices for speaking with my prospects and clients. The following are a couple that I believe are relevant in every sales situation:

Allow prospects to complete their sentences. After you've been selling the same product or service for a while, you've heard most of the common objections. The tendency is to say to yourself, "I know where they're going with this objection," and then you interrupt them mid-sentence, as if you get extra points for answering before the question is completed. You don't. You get points taken away for two reasons:

- The person doesn't feel listened to, which makes the prospect feel bad and damages your rapport with that person.
- The objection may be slightly different from person to person. Your prospect may go in a different direction. The fact that the first half of the sentence sounds familiar doesn't mean you know where the rest of the sentence is going to take the discussion.

So what should you do in this situation? I'd go so far as to say that when you hear an objection that you've heard time and time again, just pause, if only for a couple seconds. Do not immediately come up with the answer. Your prospects want to feel as if they've been heard. Some are thrilled if they are able to stump the salesperson. They really want to know that they've hit you with a real zinger and that you had to think about the answer. If you respond with an answer immediately, they'll feel defeated. It never hurts to wait a second or two before you answer.

Reframe objections with positive language. If a prospect expresses the fact that they don't have enough money to fund the project, for goodness sake resist the urge to say, "I know you don't have the money…" Instead say something like, "I understand that we'll have to be creative in making this affordable for you…" Never give more energy to an objection by repeating it.

If a prospect asks about the payback period, rather than saying, "It's three and a half years, *but* the savings-to-investment ratio is 'x,'" put a positive spin on it by saying, "It's three and a half years, *and* I think what you'll find more interesting is that the savings-to-investment ratio is 'x.'" Now, their ears are going to perk up at "…what you'll find more interesting…" and you've created an opportunity to highlight the investment you're proposing in its most positive light. Note that I use "and" rather than "but" when connecting the payback with savings-to-investment ratio, which is where I'd like to see the discussion go.

THE QUESTION TRILOGY

It's crucial to learn what your prospect needs from you before he or she is willing to buy. One of the best ways to discover this information is by asking what I call the "question trilogy:"

Question #1: "How many efficiency projects have been proposed here in the last 'x' years?" I've heard it said that there would be no music without silence between the notes. When you ask questions that require careful thought before answering, just zip it. Don't utter another word. Put your pencil to your notepad so that your prospect knows this is no time to make up stories because you're going to write down whatever answer you hear. Assuming your prospect responds that he or she had entertained proposals in the past, move on to question two.

Question #2: "How many of those projects have been approved?" Again, give your prospect time to think. After you hear the answer, move on to question three.

Question #3: "What was it about those projects that made you willing to approve them?" This is the golden question that will provide you insight into your prospect's values and decision-making processes.

The earlier in the conversation you ask these questions, the better. You might learn that you have no chance of closing a sale because the prospect is already loyal to another vendor. In this case, you should just pack up and move on to a different prospect. Or you might learn that they only work with vendors who can provide a certain service that they value. If you are able to provide them with this service, it should be front and center in your presentation going forward. Listen to what your prospect has to say, take note of it, and tailor your proposal to resonate with the answers you hear.

"The best way to prosper yourself is to prosper others."
WALTER JEWELL

SETTING LIMITS AND FRAMING COMPARISONS

Most buyers like to have choices, and they get personal satisfaction knowing that they made the right choice. That said be careful not to overwhelm your prospects with too many options. The perceived risk of making the wrong decision may become a roadblock to making any decision at all. Here are two strategies that will simplify the decision-making process for your prospects and maximize your sales:

* **Set limits**. If your company offers a wide variety of products or services, avoid offering the entire list to every prospect. Rather, customize your proposals based on what you think each prospect

will most likely prefer. Consider removing some of the available options or assembling them into groups so you can offer a choice of "Package A," "Package B," and "Package C."

- **Offer comparisons**. People like to feel as if they are getting the best value for the best price. If you offer several choices at different price levels and the highest-priced option is only slightly more expensive *and* offers the best value, your customer will almost invariably ignore the lower-priced options and select the most expensive one. They may have never considered buying the highest-priced option if the lower-priced inferior options had not been available for comparison. Realizing that most people don't actually make decisions, they make comparisons, true sales professionals arrange the selection of potential offerings in ways that maximize the probability that their prospects will make the right choice.

While we're on this topic, which do you think encourages prospects to select higher-first-cost, premium-efficiency alternatives: framing your proposals in the context of "Good, Better, Best" or "Best, Better, Good"? As you might have guessed given the manner in which I posed this question, simply reframing your alternatives as "Best, Better, Good" could actually enhance the chances of selling higher-dollar solutions. Try it for yourself the next time you're proposing a continuum of measures.

"Strive not to be a success, but rather to be of value."
ALBERT EINSTEIN

BECOME AN EXPERT IN YOUR PROSPECT'S INDUSTRY

As you're developing an understanding of your prospect's story, a good place to start would be asking yourself where you get your industry news? I'm not talking about HVAC or lighting news; I'm talking about your *prospect's* industry news. You need to do your research. Knowing that level of detail about your prospect will give you strong foundational knowledge of which dots need to be connected to build a compelling case for project approval.

- Do your research. Check out the reference section at your local library or use Google! You could also seek the guidance of a full-

service investment house that will likely have reports on various industries.

- Subscribe to and read your prospects' industry publications. It's remarkable to me how many salespeople attempt to work in segments without reading *any* of their prospects' trade magazines or newsletters.

- Attend your *prospects'* conferences—and not just to network. If you can't attend, go online afterward and see if you can download (or purchase from a third party) a copy of the conference agenda, recordings of the general session, PowerPoints and/or handouts from the presenters, etc. You'll learn what the industry is interested in, who the big dogs and opinion leaders are, what the industry sees as its challenges, and much more—all of which constitutes great fodder for finding dots to connect.

- Understand the metrics that matter to your prospects. Hint: It's not likely to be kilowatt-hours or therms.

- Take time to understand how your product or service fits their business. If you do this, three things will happen:
  - You'll have much more interesting conversations with your prospects—in fact, they'll enjoy the conversations more because they will be grounded in *their* reality, not yours.
  - You'll be better able to introduce and connect dots that point inarguably to the value of your offering.
  - Your closing ratio will increase because you will be offering benefits that resonate with goals your prospects are already seeking.

- Think systems, not pieces. Throughout this whole exercise, resist the temptation to focus only on your piece of the puzzle. Think business systems. Equipment systems. Decision-making systems. Remember, you're not just competing against other energy projects. You are competing for time and capital with *every other initiative* your prospect could be evaluating in addition to the one you are proposing.

- Find out what matters most—and then find a way to connect some attribute of what you offer to the dots that your prospects most value.
- Ask prospects (or current customers) if you can do a "ride along."
- Put yourself in their shoes. Ask yourself, "Why would you do business with you?"

"A constant, unproductive preoccupation with all the things we have to do is the single largest consumer of time and energy."
KERRY GLEESON

SELLING BEYOND THE OBVIOUS

Every efficiency-related product or service has a direct benefit for the consumer. However, true sales professionals take the next step, transcending those direct benefits and highlighting the additional positive impacts. Take foam weather stripping, for example. The most obvious benefit of foam weather stripping is a warmer home (assuming it's installed in a cold climate). Are you going to close a sale every time by telling your prospect that your product will result in a warmer home? Probably not.

I was recently asked to coach the sales team of a company that provides weather stripping and other energy measures to low-income homeowners on a direct-install basis. To prepare for that engagement, I did a little research on the downstream advantages of energy efficiency for low-income housing. Applied to the example of weather stripping, here's what I found:

When you put the weather stripping in, you prevent a cold living room. When you prevent a cold living room, the kids are no longer embarrassed to bring their friends over. If the kids aren't embarrassed to bring their friends over, they're not on the streets getting into trouble. Moreover, what comes in with the cold air? Moisture. What problem does the moisture cause? In many cases, mold. What happens once the mold arrives? It causes asthma. What problem does asthma cause? Sick kids. What happens when kids get sick? Parents miss work to keep kids out of school. What happens when those parents miss too many days of work? They lose their jobs. What happens then? It goes all the way down…

So are you selling foam rubber or are you selling the prevention of any one of those impacts of not having the right weather stripping in the house? You'll have a much more interesting conversation if you discuss the in-depth impacts rather than just selling on the idea that weather stripping keeps the prospect's house warmer.

Customers have limited time. You need to connect the dots for them. I can assure you that most of the decision-makers, and even the influencers, that you encounter will not have spent nearly as much time as you have understanding how energy efficiency intersects with what they value most. Your job is to know their segment well enough so that you can actually connect the dots for them.

FINDING GREAT LEADS FOR YOUR PRODUCT OR SERVICE

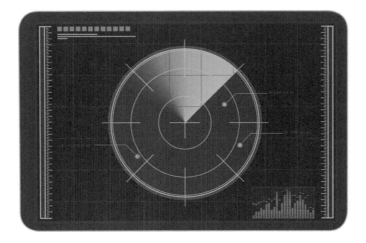

- Embrace and cultivate *all* of the empowering qualities of a sales professional.
- Commit to being proactive rather than reactive.
- Learn to leverage those who sell to your typical prospects before and after you do.
  - ◇ Property managers who need to field and address all of those "hot/cold" calls from disgruntled occupants.
  - ◇ Building engineering firms that have to operate the aging equipment you should be replacing.

- ◇ Mechanical contractors who have to service equipment long past its estimated lifetime.
- ◇ Other suppliers who provide parts for aging equipment.
- ◇ Air balancing firms, duct cleaning firms, etc.
- ◇ Real estate brokers with knowledge of thermal comfort, noise, and other shortcomings in the buildings they know well.
- • Think carefully about your ideal prospects and build a profile to begin pursuing today.
- • Take the time to build the tools you'll need to open doors and keep them open.
- • Get organized and automated so that you can keep up with the surge of sales activity you're about to experience.

"A man must be big enough to admit his mistakes, smart enough to profit from them, and strong enough to correct them."
JOHN C. MAXWELL

EMBRACING THE INTANGIBLE

When you sell energy efficiency, you're selling a high-dollar intangible. Whether or not you can physically touch the chiller or the LED lights or the solar film or whatever, you're essentially selling an intangible because your customers aren't really buying metal chillers, LED circuit boards, or plastic films. They're buying the concept that their lives will be better in the wake of installing these technologies. If that perspective is true—and believe me, it is—you have to ask yourself, "How are other intangibles sold?"

Consider a vacation, for example. Is that a tangible or an intangible good? Can you touch a vacation? Can you feel it? How is a vacation sold? Do they give you the size of the room or the speed of your cruise ship? No.

They give you all sorts of emotional images about *how much better you're going to feel* once you're on vacation.

Let's get back to the energy world. Assume you're selling solar panels to a homeowner. You can tell your prospect, "If you install these solar panels on your home, you'll save $1,000 a year on your electric bills" and hope for the best.

Or, you could continue, "Think about it. That's like giving yourself an after-tax raise of $1,000 a year. How much would you pay today to guarantee yourself $1,000 in increased after-tax annual income (plus inflation!) for the next twenty years, which happens to be the predicted useful life of these solar panels?"

In fact, you could kick it up a notch, as Chef Emeril Lagasse is fond of saying on the Food Network. What is the *before-tax* value of that $1,000 raise? At a 35 percent marginal tax bracket, it's more like $1,500 per year (plus inflation). So now your question becomes, "How much would you pay today for a $1,500 (before-tax) increase in your annual salary (plus inflation) for the next twenty years?"

Your prospect will undoubtedly get the point—the value of that increased income over the next twenty years is greater than the cost of the panels… and a whole lot sexier than the thought of saving about $80 per month on the electric bill.

Forget talking about equipment specifications. Instead, ask questions that evoke an emotional response. Selling an intangible is all about reframing the sale in a way that allows your prospect to grab onto something that is tangible, something that they can visualize, something to which they can become emotionally attached.

IT'S ALL ABOUT ATTITUDE

There's a significant correlation between positive attitude and sales performance. If you look at sales performance data, you'll probably notice that people are most likely to make a new sale immediately after they've just made one. Why does this happen? Because a successful sale boosts your general outlook and attitude, and that emotional lift makes you a more effective sales professional.

What's also interesting is that many salespeople alternate between great sales months and lousy ones. This pattern can also be explained by attitude. After a great month with back-to-back sales, one might rejoice, "Woo-hoo! What a great month! Now I can relax a bit." There's only one problem: As soon as you relax, you run the danger of falling into a slump. You stop doing the blocking and tackling. You stop making the cold calls. You stop being responsive. And then all of a sudden, you're in panic mode: "Oh my gosh, I'm really behind on my numbers. I now have to scratch my way up to the top of the mountain again." That desperation actually *delays* your next sale. Prospects can sense it in your voice, which can unnecessarily elongate the trough of suboptimal performance. Moreover, once you finally do work your way back up to the top, you may very well repeat the cycle, unless you're vigilant about the perils of doing so.

You can make *every* month a great sales month, provided you keep a positive attitude and never rest on your laurels.

"Failure is instructive. The person who really thinks learns quite as much from his failures as from his successes."

JOHN DEWEY

THE SIMPLE POWER OF
A SINGLE DAY...

Seth Godin once wrote a blog on the simple power of a single day… how taking just one small action each and every day could yield monumental change by the end of a year. This philosophy applies to any part of your life. It certainly applies to improving your sales skills.

Here are ten small steps you can take to bring you closer to becoming an efficiency sales professional:

1. Get all of your "To-Do" items out of your head.
2. Develop a profile for your ideal prospect.

3. Create a template for collecting information to go into your proposal or report.
4. Map the decision-makers of your target customer.
5. Research and register for four networking events this month—and resolve to arrive at each one early and stay late (the middle gets crowded).
6. Set up your LinkedIn profile (or make it more robust).
7. Obtain a testimonial from a previous client.
8. Send a handwritten "Thank You!" note.
9. Create a vision board depicting your goals and dreams.
10. Call a previous customer and ask why he or she bought from you.

Doing any one of these actions just once may not change your life. However, committing to performing one (or more) of these simple actions each day will definitely put you on the pathway to becoming a true efficiency sales professional.

"Don't make friends who are comfortable to be with. Make friends that will force you to level yourself up."
THOMAS J. WATSON

NEXT STEPS

The Efficiency Sales Professional Institute provides training, coaching, and resources focused on addressing three acupressure points we see in the efficiency market today:

- Benchmarking, which prepares building owners and the solutions providers who serve them to measure, manage, and lead.
- Efficiency-focused professional selling, which is vital for capturing attention, advancing compelling proposals, and facilitating approvals.
- Financial analysis, which allows efficiency professionals to migrate the conversation from myths to the math and motivation needed to secure project approvals.

Whether we provide in-person or online courses, custom training, keynotes, or coaching, we know we've accomplished our goal when our audience leaves informed, re-energized, and ready to take action.

Selling Energy: Inspiring Ideas That Help Get Projects Approved! may be your entry point into the world of efficiency-focused professional selling. If so, you'd do well to visit SellingEnergy.com and think about taking the next step in your professional development.

If you've already availed yourself of some of our other offerings, this book will complement those trainings and provide valuable "drip-irrigation" content reinforcement to help you apply what you've already learned.

Many who attend our training sessions distribute this book broadly throughout their own organizations—or recommend it to their trading partners—to help ensure that all parties collaborate more effectively in getting more projects approved.

If you're not already a subscriber to our daily Jewell Insights™ blog, visit www.eefg.com to sign up for the email version, which is available in daily or weekly digest format. Alternatively, you can search the Apple or Google Play store to download our mobile app to your smartphone. As of this writing, we have thousands of regular readers and hundreds of testimonials affirming that the wisdom we share in Jewell Insights has helped increase closing ratios and shorten sales cycles. It's a wonderful and free resource to help you advance efficiency.

If you have feedback to share on our book or other training offerings, or want to learn how we can help you advance your own initiatives, please contact us at info@eefg.com.

ESP NINJA™ APP

The Efficiency Sales Professional™ (ESP™) Certificate Program is 48 hours of training on sales, efficiency, financial analysis, and personal productivity that will help you become an efficiency sales "ninja" and turbocharge your success.

Our ESP Ninja™ app is your 365-day portal into the world of efficiency-focused professional selling. Authored by Mark Jewell, co-founder of the Efficiency Sales Professional Institute, this free app delivers "drip-irrigation" content reinforcement of the principles contained in the ESP™ curriculum.

Enjoy insightful articles, informative videos, and inspirational quotes that will help you move efficiency forward. If your success depends on your ability to advance efficiency initiatives, this app is for you. We guarantee a stream of high-quality content at your fingertips. Please feel free to pass it along to your colleagues and clients as well.

SELLINGENERGY.COM

SellingEnergy.com allows you to experience our training wherever and whenever you'd like. This content is available online/on-demand and can be viewed on a PC, Mac, iPad, or smartphone. View the content you want. Repeat a lesson if you wish. Revisit the material when you're ready to apply it.

We focus on teaching people how to drive efficiency by connecting the dots for decision-makers. Our training is designed to get attendees to take action, to identify and approve more projects, to increase participation in incentive programs, to post greater energy savings, and to make their (or their customers') operations more competitive, profitable, and valuable.

Each of our courses delivers insights and skills that make attendees more successful the very next day.

The Efficiency Sales Professional Institute and its SellingEnergy.com online store exist to create efficiency sales ninjas who:

- Find the highest-value targets and capture their attention.
- Map the decision-making chain and skillfully assess motivations.
- Concisely communicate value and artfully blend emotion and logic to neutralize objections.
- Replace myths with math and escape the clutches of simple payback period.
- Perform in ways that achieve results and merit emulation.

The Efficiency Sales Professional Institute and SellingEnergy.com are operated by Energy Efficiency Funding Group (EEFG), Inc. EEFG is a Continuing Education Systems Registered Provider through the American Institute of Architects (AIA) and an approved education provider by the Green Building Certification Institute (GBCI) for the LEED Credential Maintenance Program (CMP).

CPSIA information can be obtained at www.ICGtesting.com
Printed in the USA
LVOW01*0952120914

403789LV00012B/21/P